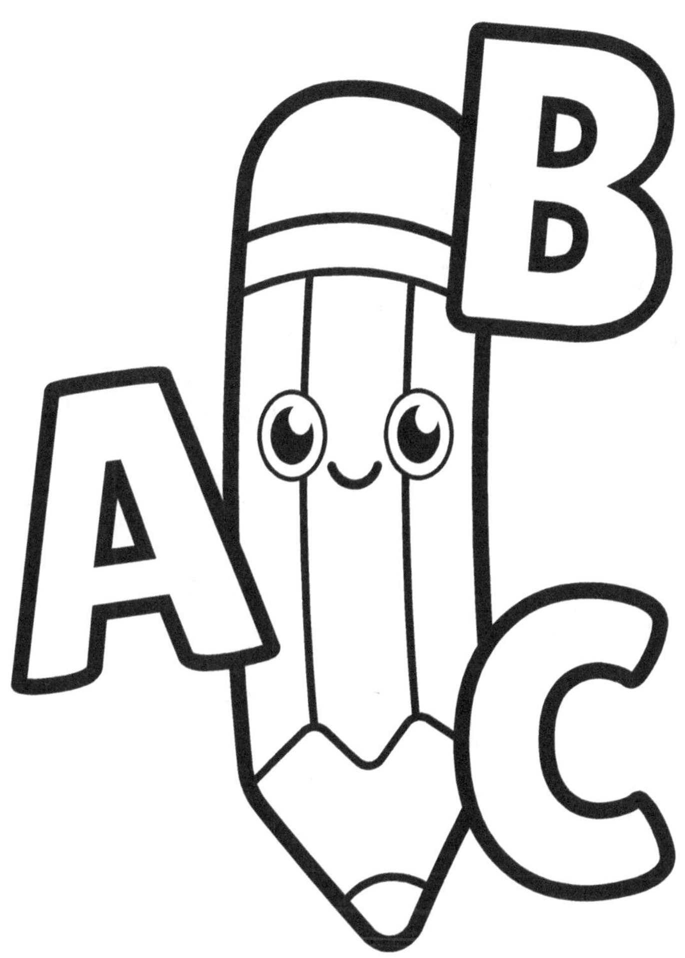

THIS BOOK BELONGS TO

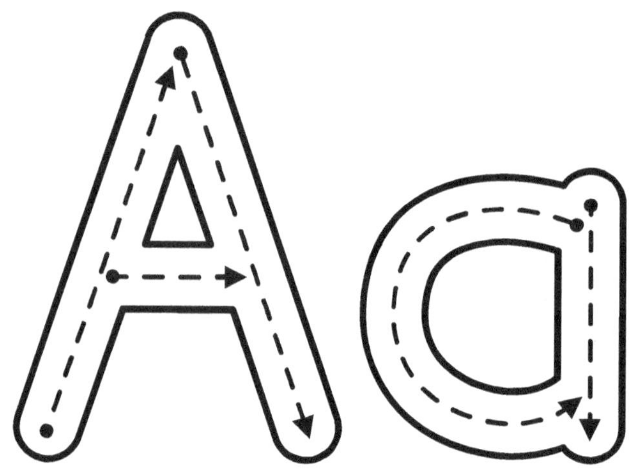

Trace The Letter - Aa

Circle The Letter - A

C D A F

B E H G

I M L J

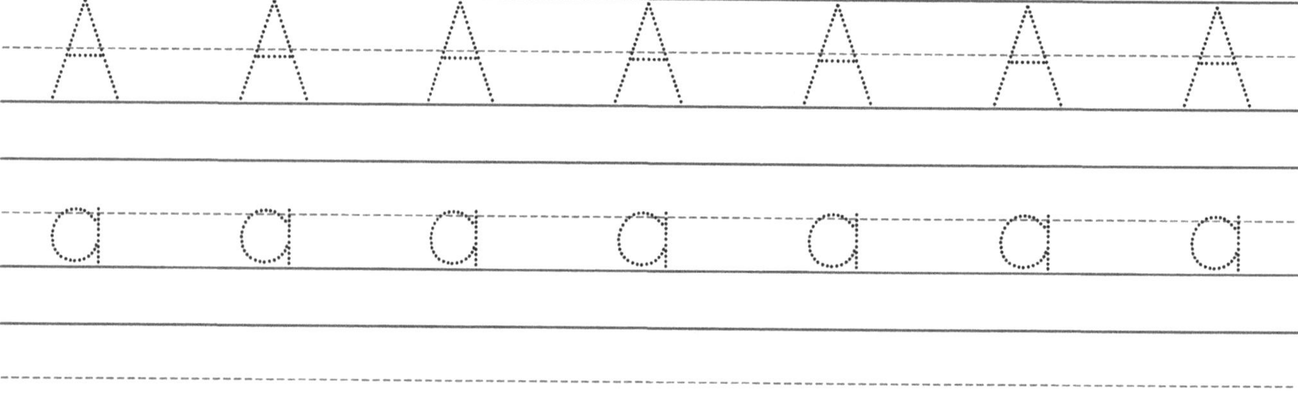

Write The Missing Letter

	B	C	D
E	F	G	H
I	J	K	L

Color And Trace

Apple

<table>
<tr><td>A B C</td><td>PRACTICE TIME</td></tr>
</table>

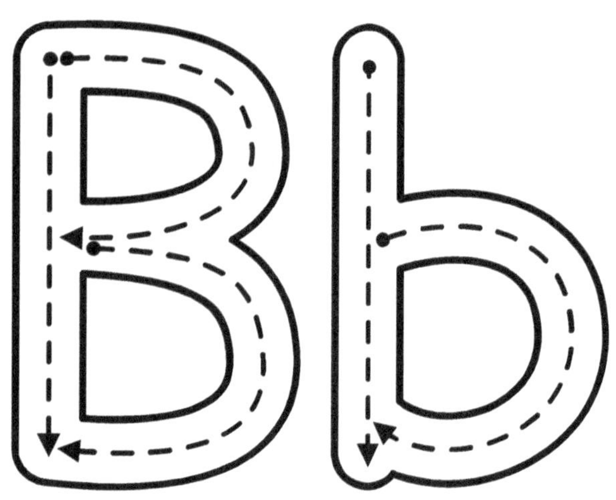

Trace The Letter - Bb

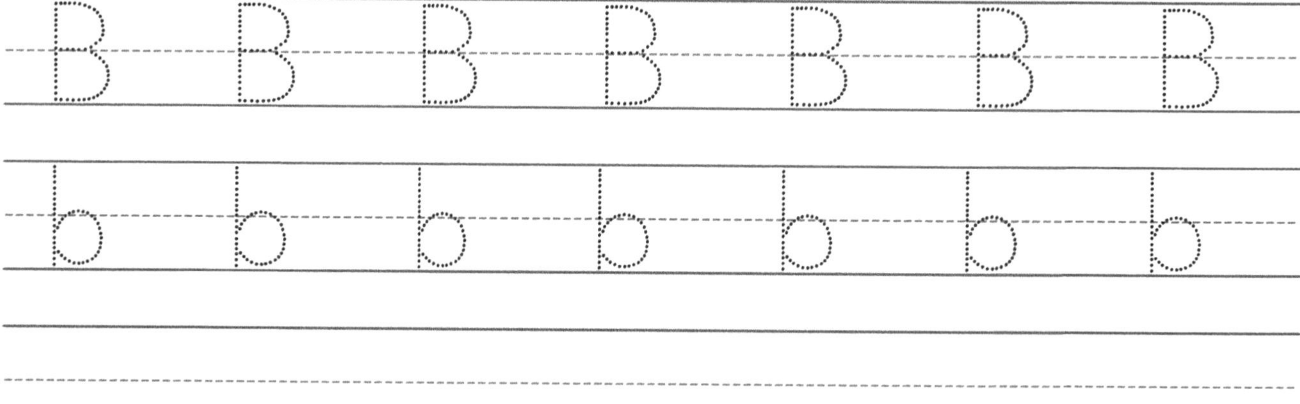

Write The Missing Letter

Color And Trace

Ball

<table><tr><td>A B C</td><td># PRACTICE TIME</td></tr></table>

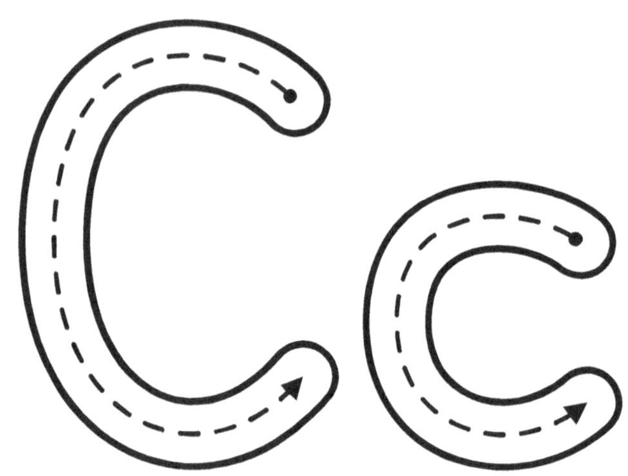

Circle The Letter - C

K D A F

B E H G

I C L J

Trace The Letter - Cc

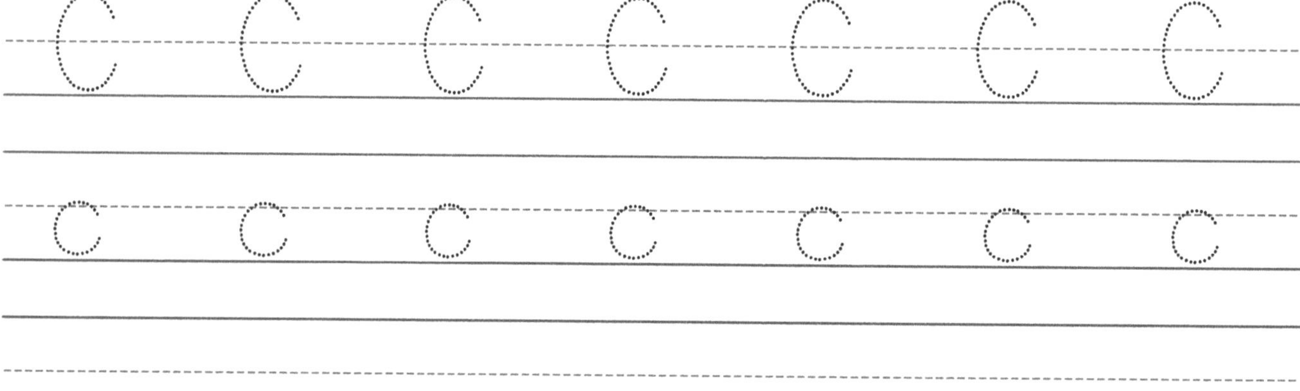

Write The Missing Letter

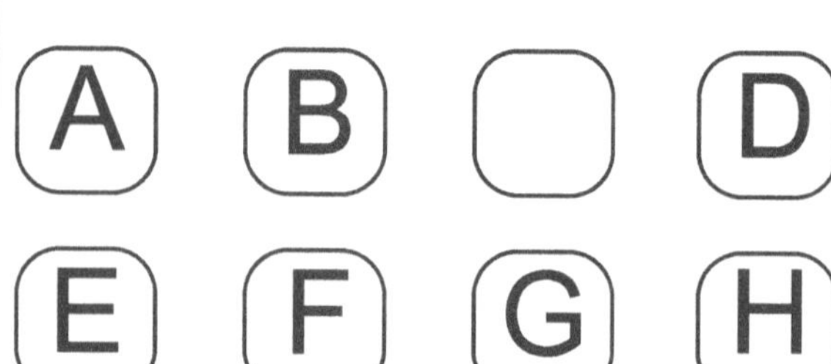

A	B		D
E	F	G	H
I	J	K	L

Color And Trace

Cat

<table><tr><td>A B C</td><td><h1 style="text-align:center">PRACTICE TIME</h1></td></tr></table>

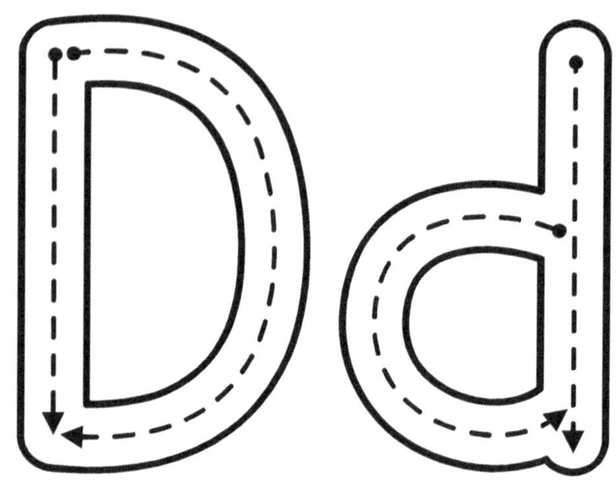

Trace The Letter - Dd

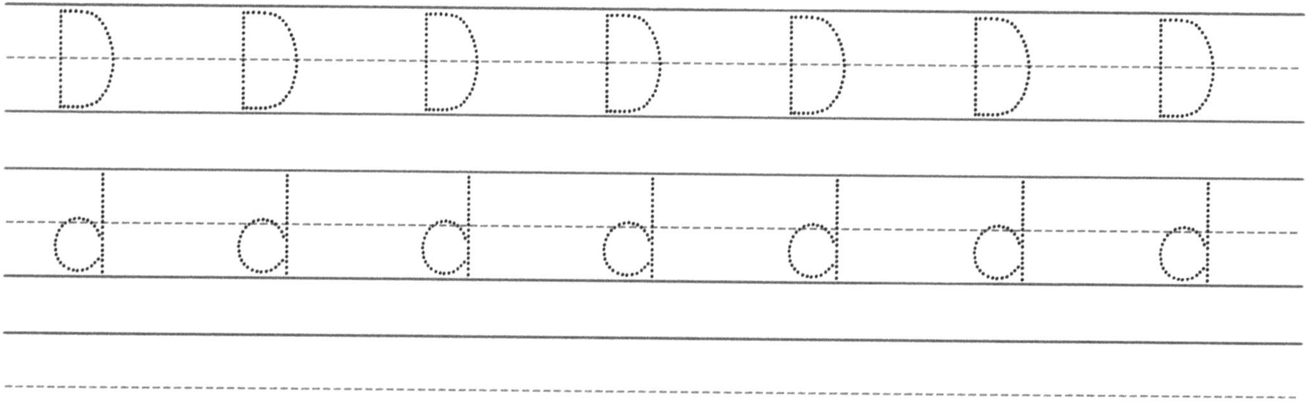

Write The Missing Letter

Color And Trace

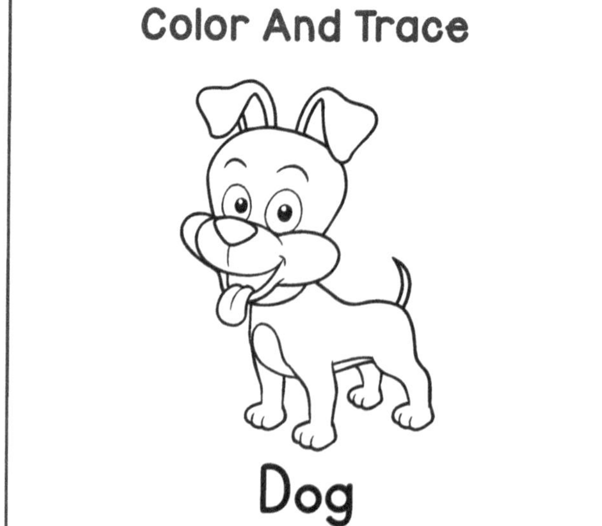

Dog

<table><tr><td>A B C</td><td>PRACTICE TIME</td></tr></table>

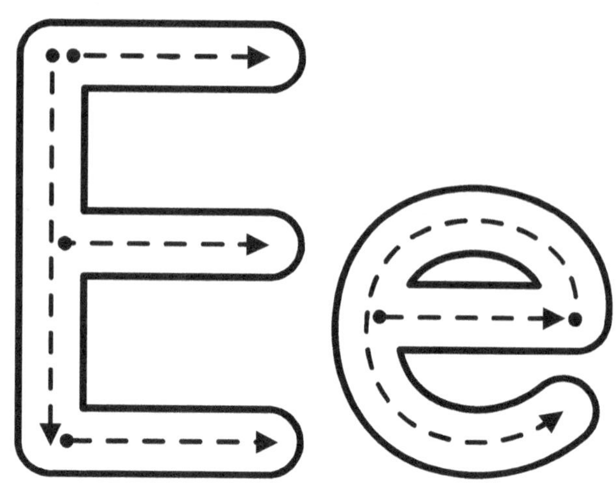

Trace The Letter - Ee

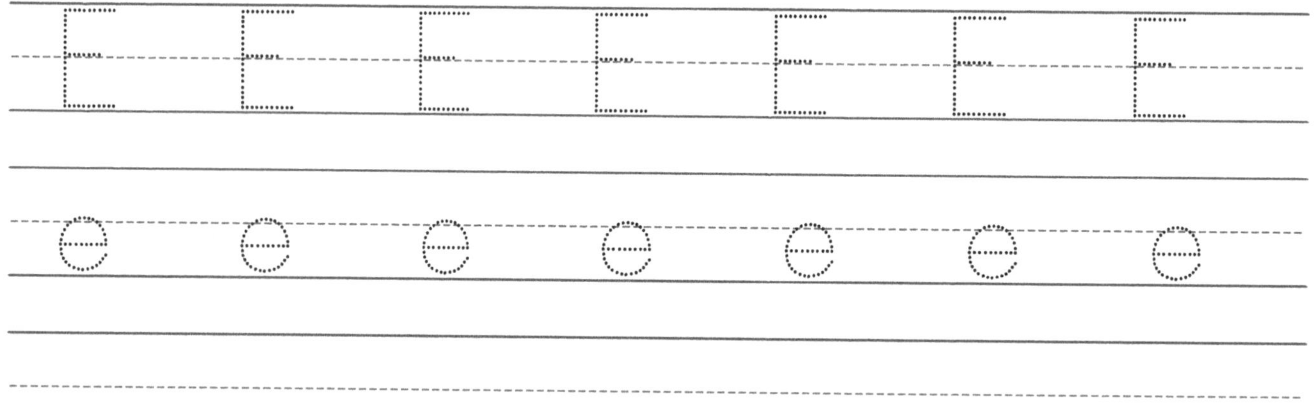

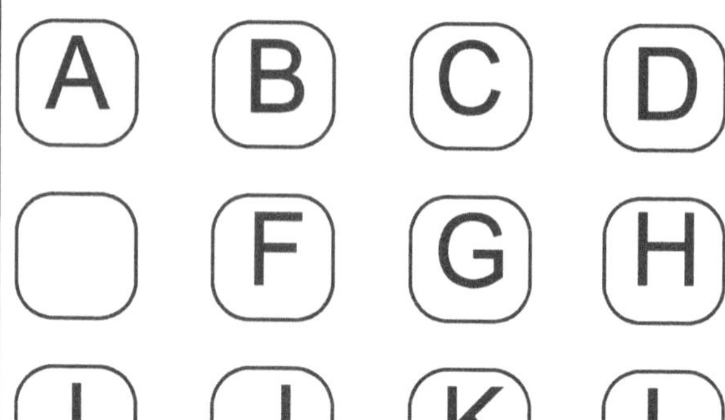

Write The Missing Letter

A	B	C	D
	F	G	H
I	J	K	L

Color And Trace

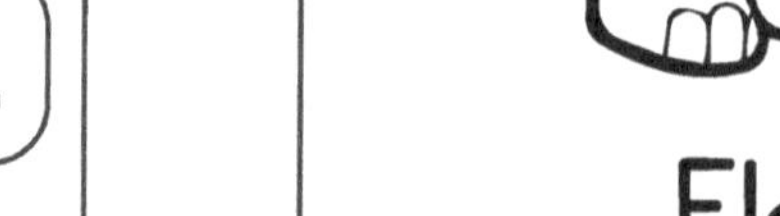

Elephant

<table><tr><td>A B C</td><td><h1>PRACTICE TIME</h1></td></tr></table>

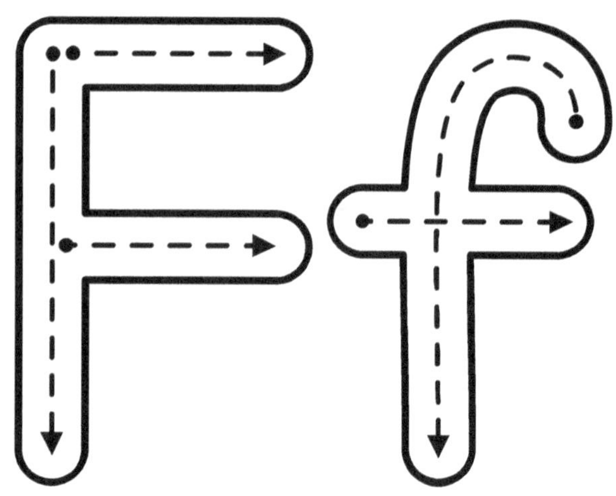

Trace The Letter - Ff

Circle The Letter - F

K D A F
B E H G
I C L J

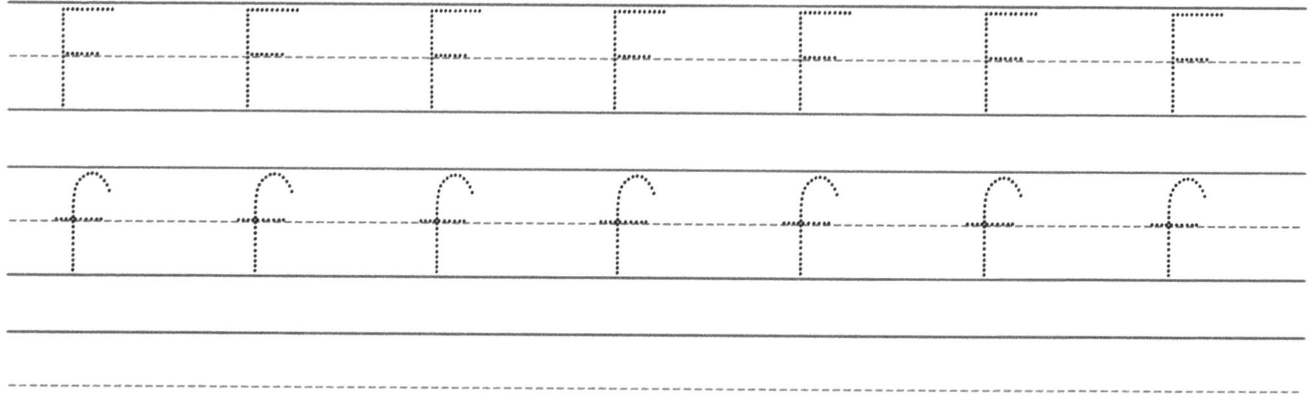

Write The Missing Letter

A | B | C | D
E | | G | H
I | J | K | L

Color And Trace

Fox

<table><tr><td>A B C</td><td>PRACTICE TIME</td></tr></table>

Circle The Letter - G

K D A F
B E H G
I C L J

Trace The Letter - Gg

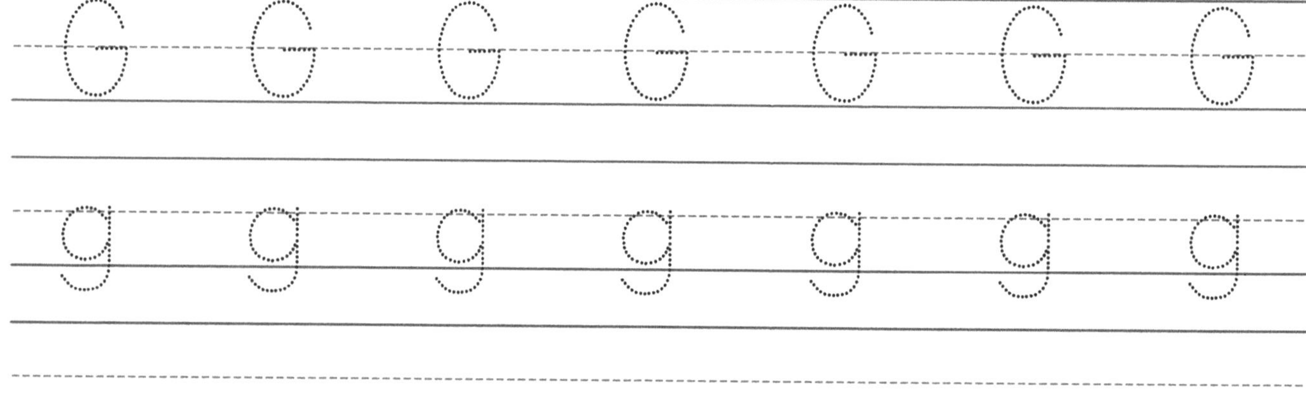

Write The Missing Letter

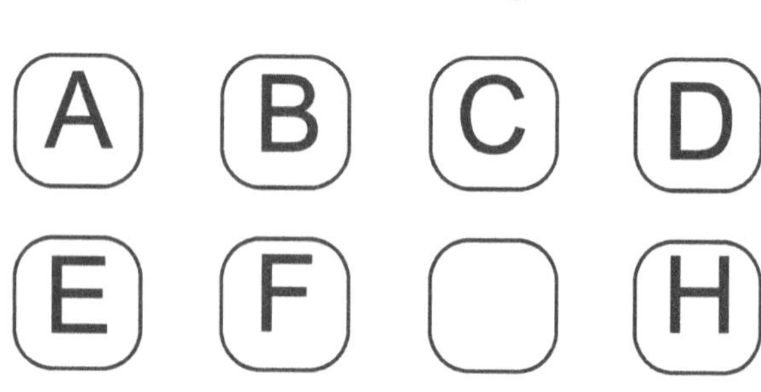

Color And Trace

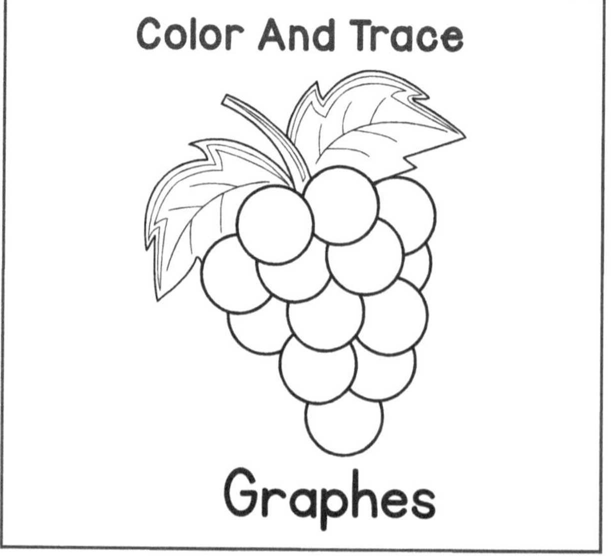

Graphes

<table><tr><td>A B C</td><td>PRACTICE TIME</td></tr></table>

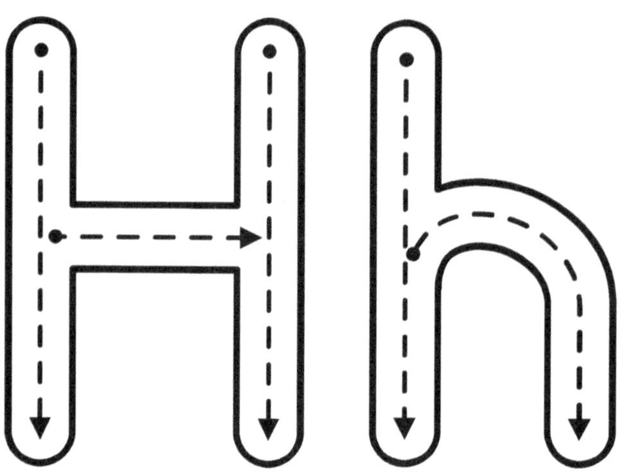

Trace The Letter - Hh

Circle The Letter - H

K D A F
B E H G
I C L J

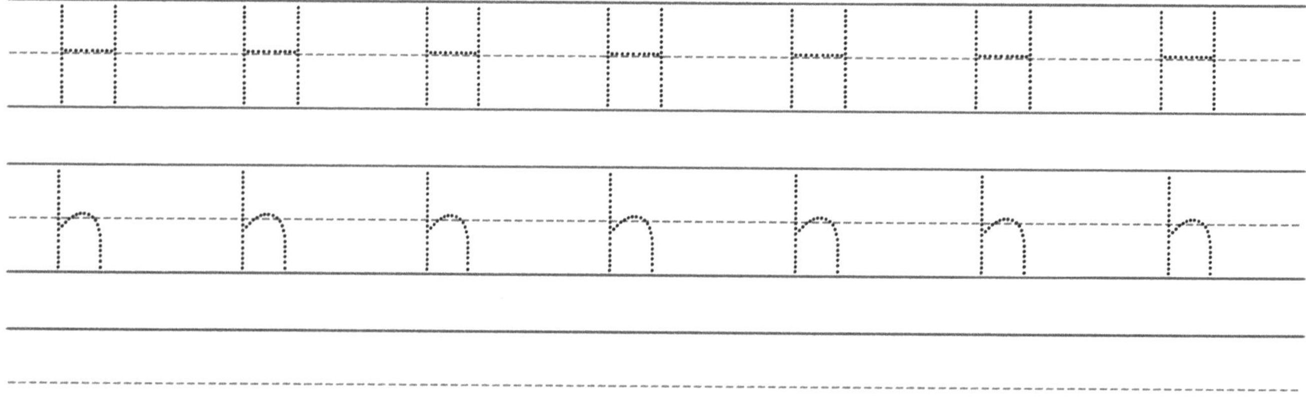

Write The Missing Letter

 A  B  C  D

 E  F  G

 I  J  K L

Color And Trace

Horse

<table><tr><td>A B C</td><td>PRACTICE TIME</td></tr></table>

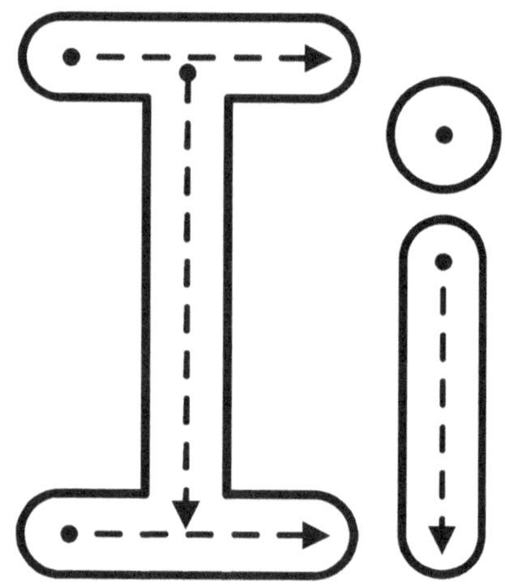

Trace The Letter - Ii

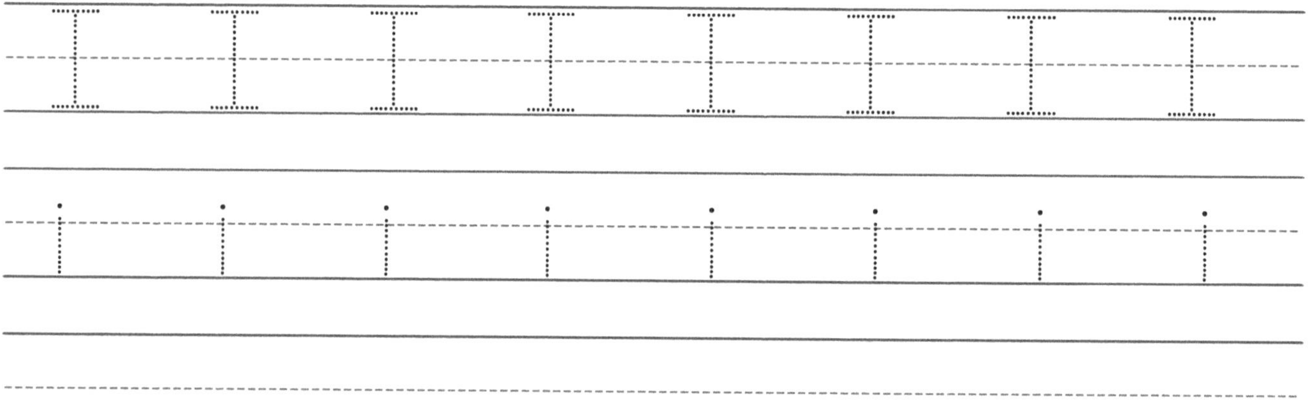

Write The Missing Letter

 A  B  C 

 E  F  G 

  J  K 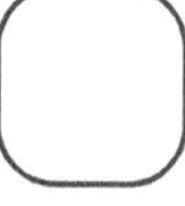

Color And Trace

Insect

<table><tr><td>A B C</td><td>PRACTICE TIME</td></tr></table>

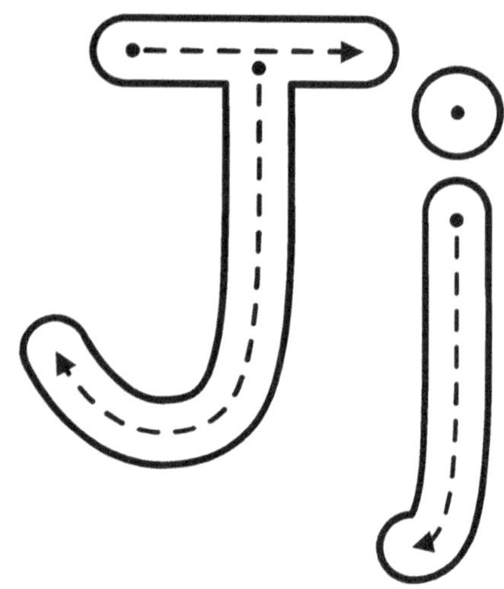

Trace The Letter - Jj

Circle The Letter - J

K D A F

B E H G

I C L J

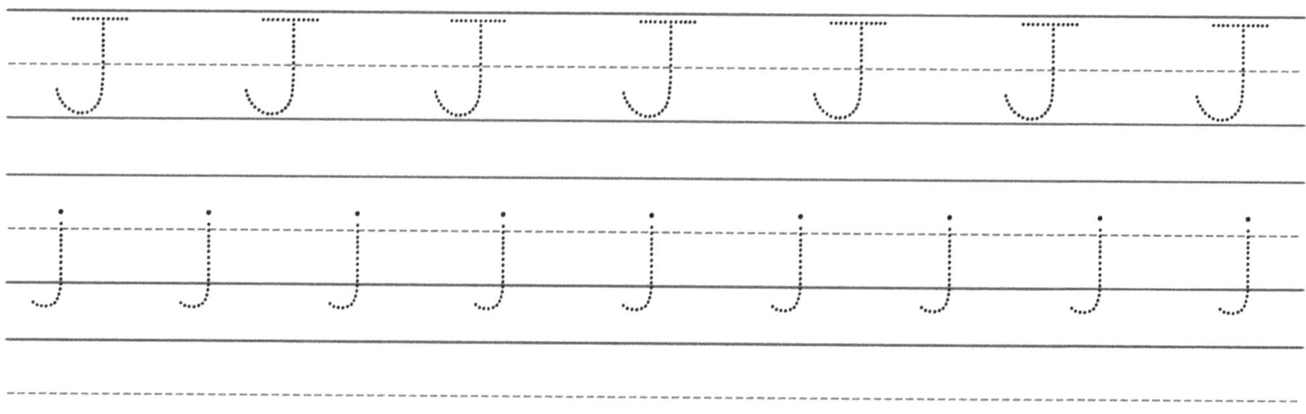

Write The Missing Letter

A	B	C	D
E	F	G	H
I		K	L

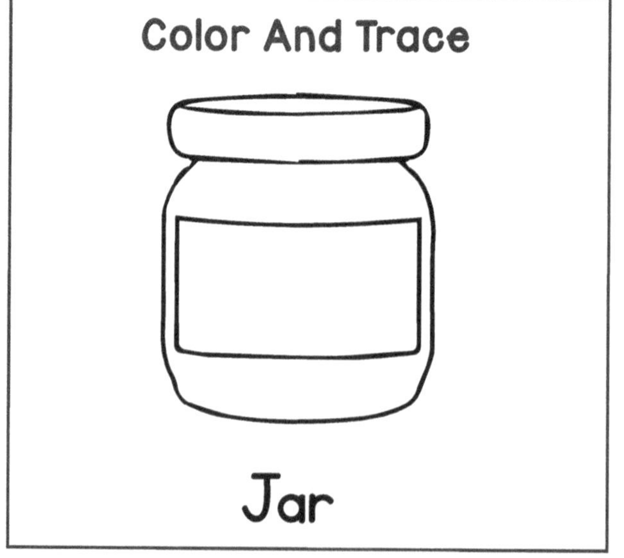

Color And Trace

Jar

<table><tr><td>A B C</td><td><h1>PRACTICE TIME</h1></td></tr></table>

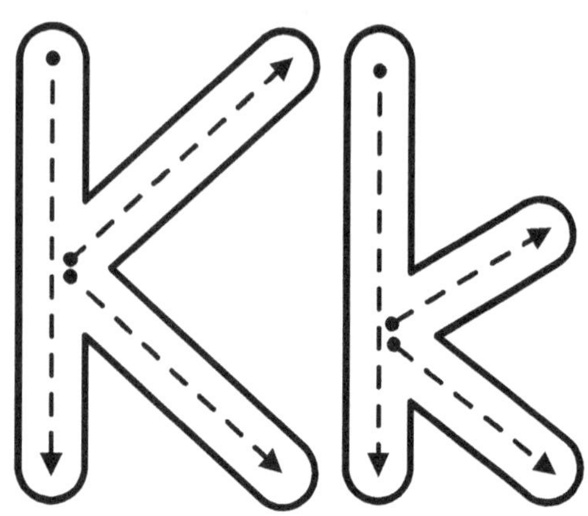

Trace The Letter - Kk

Circle The Letter - K

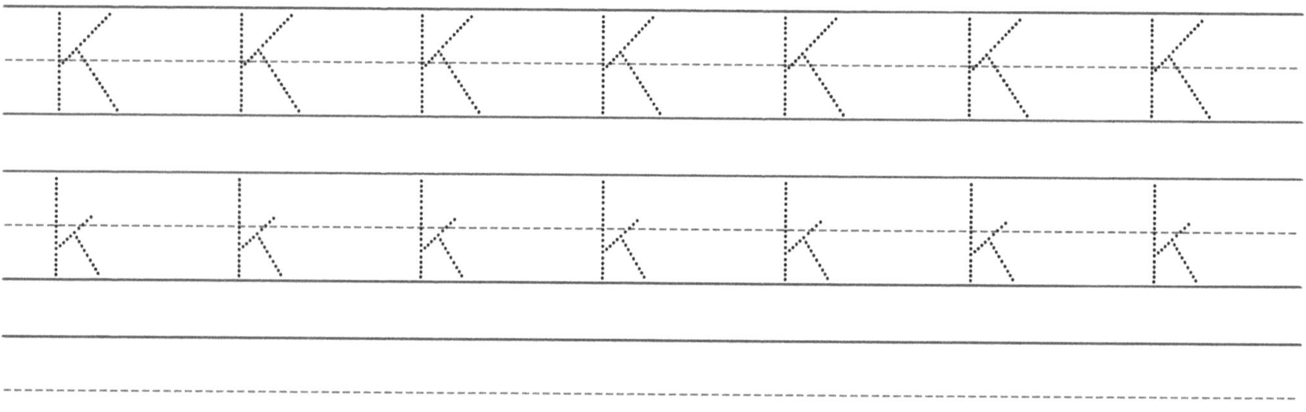

K K K K K K K K

k k k k k k k k

Write The Missing Letter

Color And Trace

King

A B C PRACTICE TIME

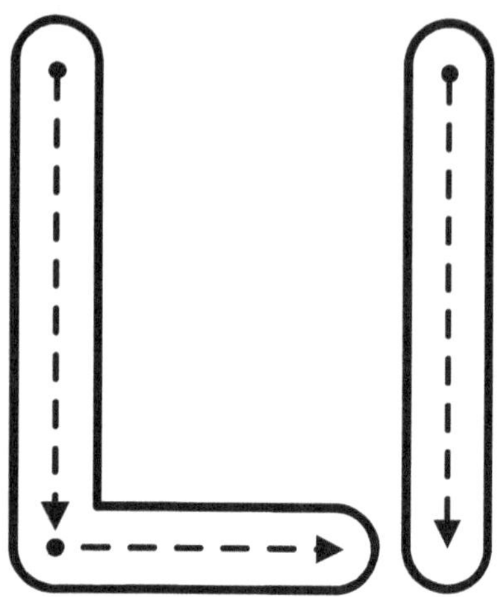

Trace The Letter - Ll

Circle The Letter - L

K D A F

B E H G

I C L J

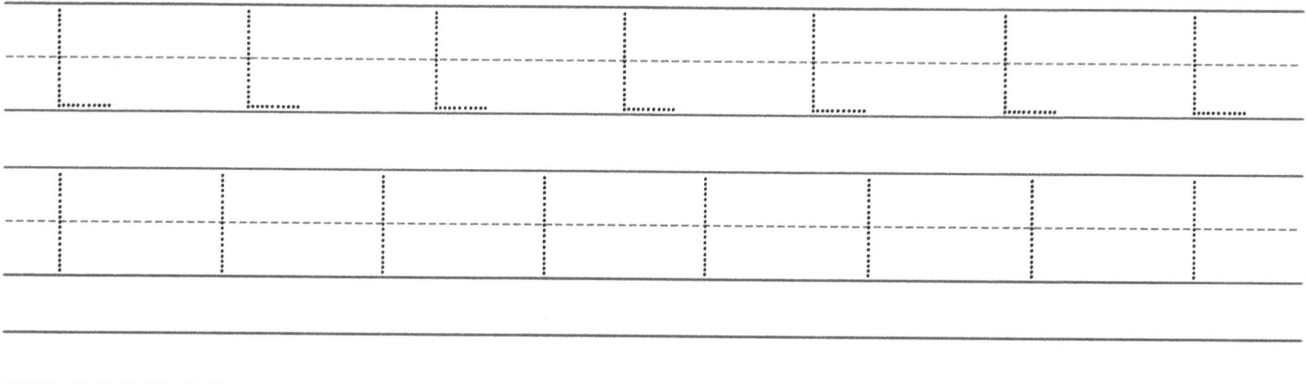

Write The Missing Letter

Color And Trace

Lion

<table><tr><td>A B C</td><td>PRACTICE TIME</td></tr></table>

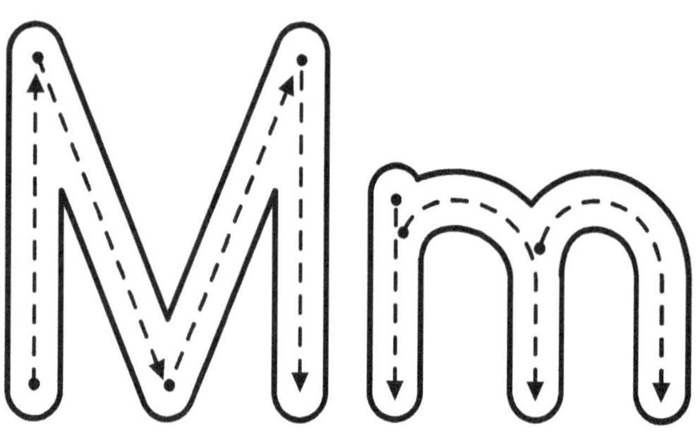

Circle The Letter - M

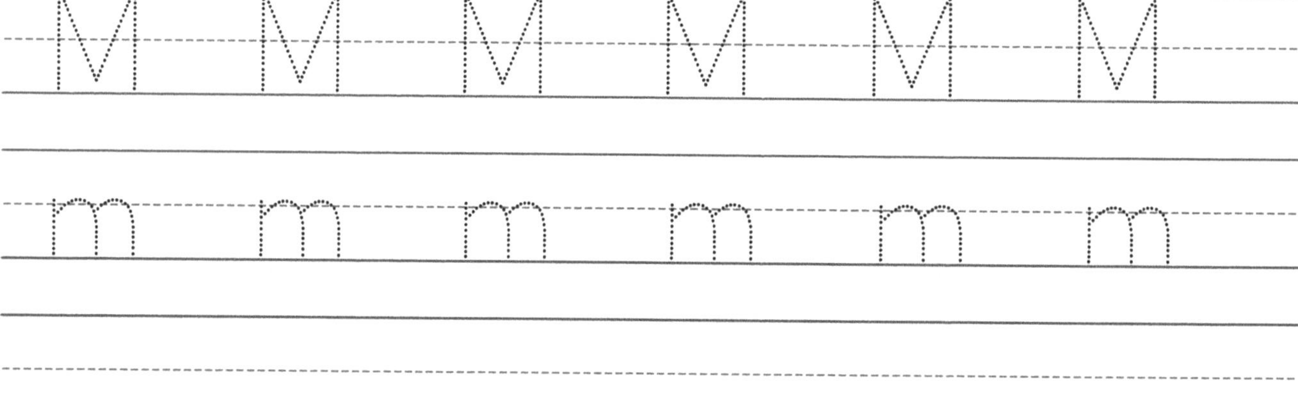

P D T O

R M I Q

V N S U

Trace The Letter - Mm

M M M M M M M

m m m m m m m

Write The Missing Letter

  N  O  P

Q R S T

U V W X

Color And Trace

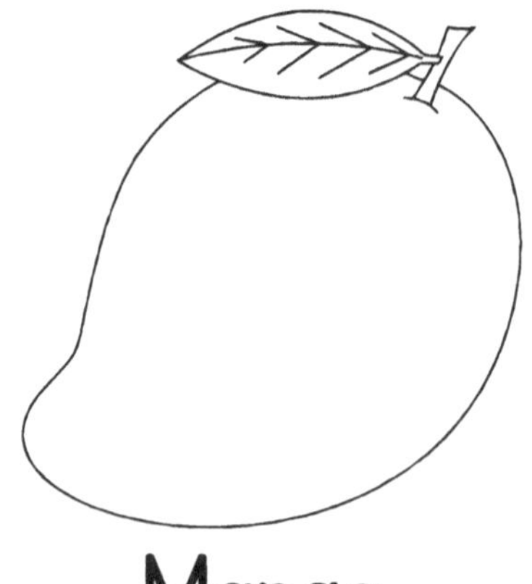

Mango

A B C | PRACTICE TIME

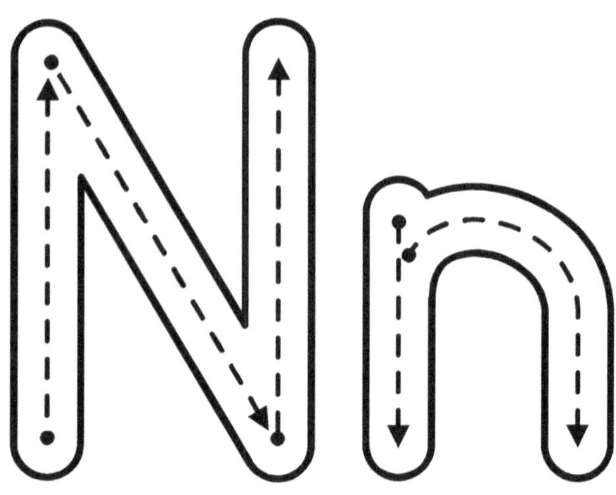

Trace The Letter - Nn

Circle The Letter - N

P D T O

R M I Q

V N S U

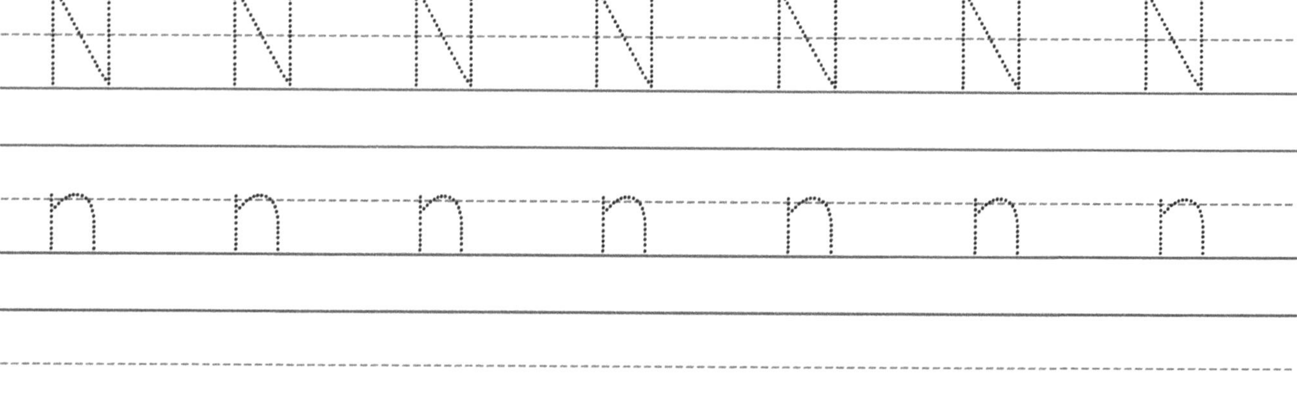

Write The Missing Letter

 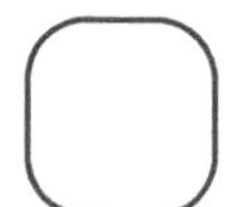  

M		O	P
Q	R	S	T
U	V	W	X

Color And Trace

Nest

<table>
<tr><td>A B C</td><td><h1>PRACTICE TIME</h1></td></tr>
</table>

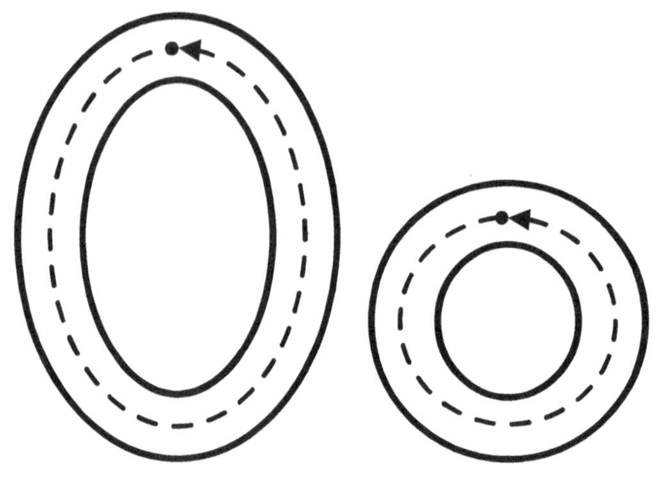

Trace The Letter - Oo

Circle The Letter - O

P D T O

R M I Q

V N S U

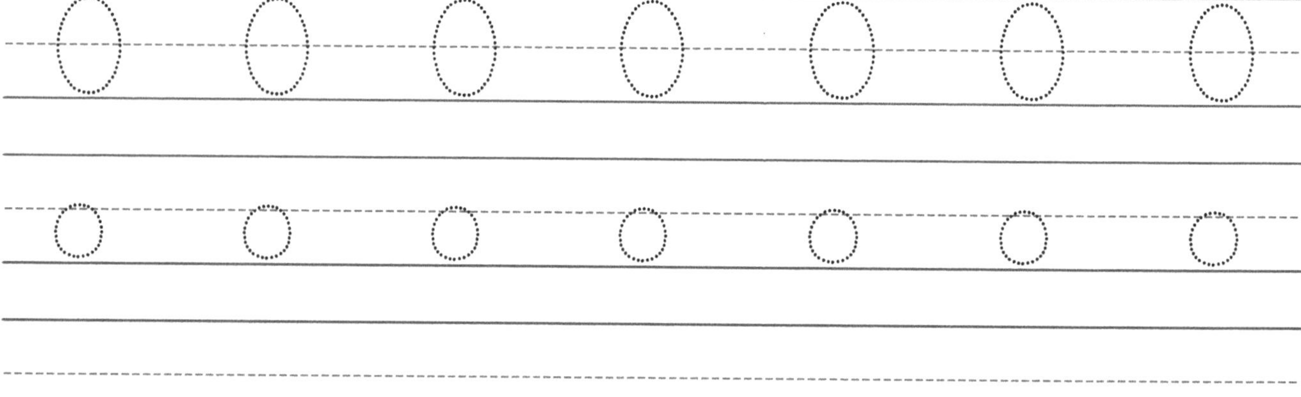

Write The Missing Letter

M	N		P
Q	R	S	T
U	V	W	X

Color And Trace

Onion

<table><tr><td>A B C</td><td>PRACTICE TIME</td></tr></table>

<table><tr><td>A B C</td><td>

TRACING ALPHABETS
</td></tr></table>

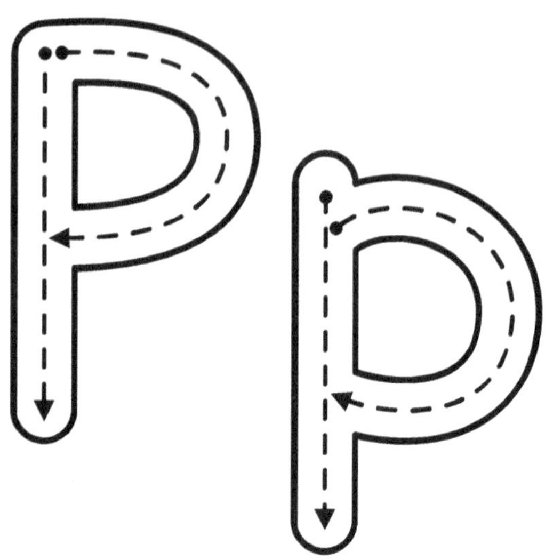

Trace The Letter - Pp

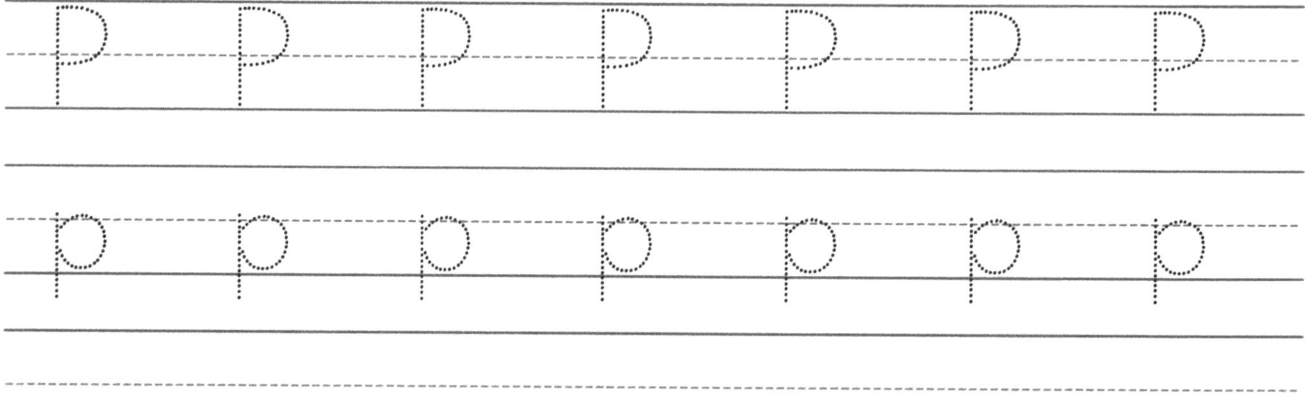

Write The Missing Letter

M	N	O	
Q	R	S	T
U	V	W	X

Color And Trace

Pig

<table><tr><td>A B C</td><td>PRACTICE TIME</td></tr></table>

Trace The Letter - Qq

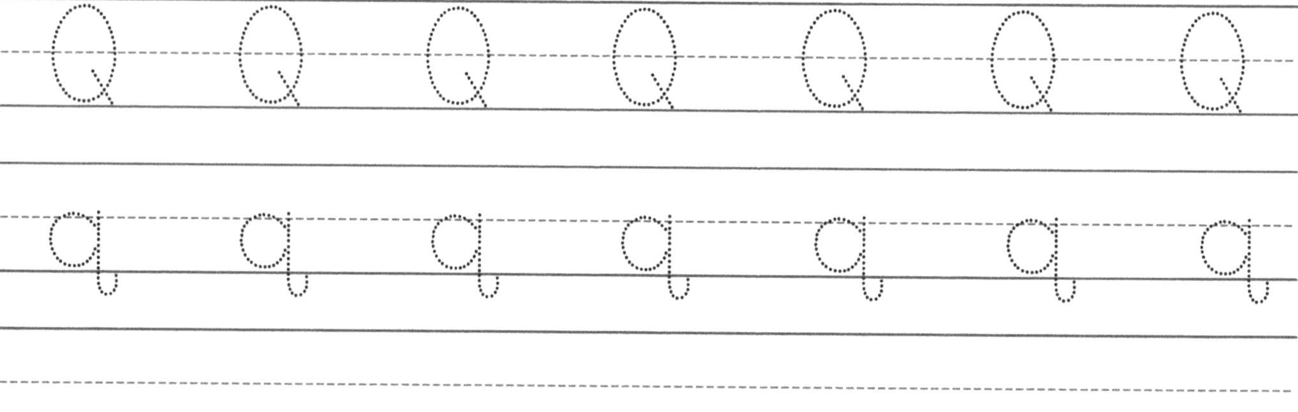

Circle The Letter - Q

P D T O

R M I Q

V N S U

Write The Missing Letter

M N O P

R S T

U V W X

Color And Trace

Queen

<table><tr><td>A B C</td><td><h1 align="center">PRACTICE TIME</h1></td></tr></table>

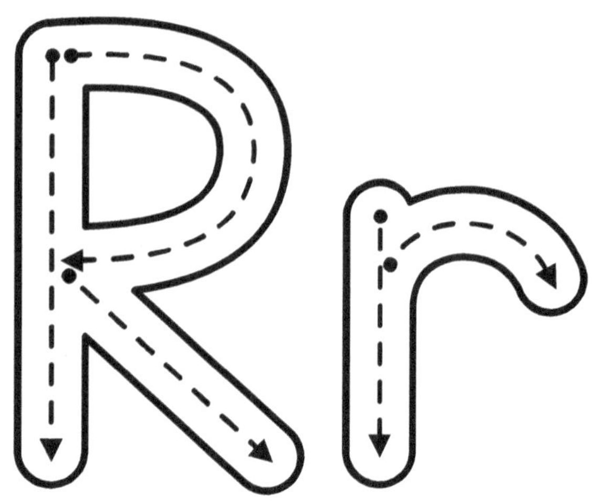

Trace The Letter - Rr

Circle The Letter - R

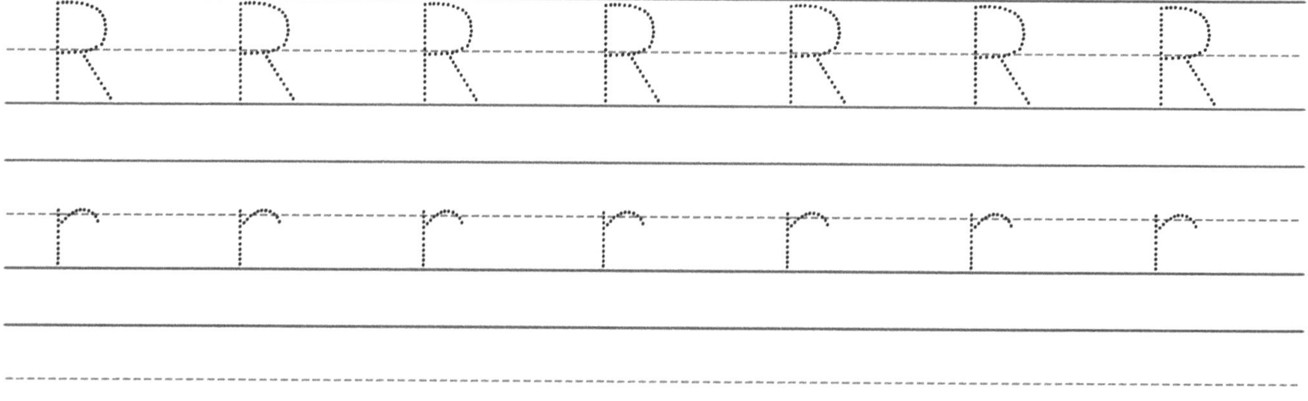

P D T O
R M I Q
V N S U

R R R R R R R

r r r r r r r

Write The Missing Letter

M N O P

Q S T

U V W X

Color And Trace

Rat

<table><tr><td>A B C</td><td><h1>PRACTICE TIME</h1></td></tr></table>

Trace The Letter - Ss

Circle The Letter - S

P D T O
R M I Q
V N S U

Write The Missing Letter

Color And Trace

Shark

<table><tr><td>**A B C**</td><td><h1>PRACTICE TIME</h1></td></tr></table>

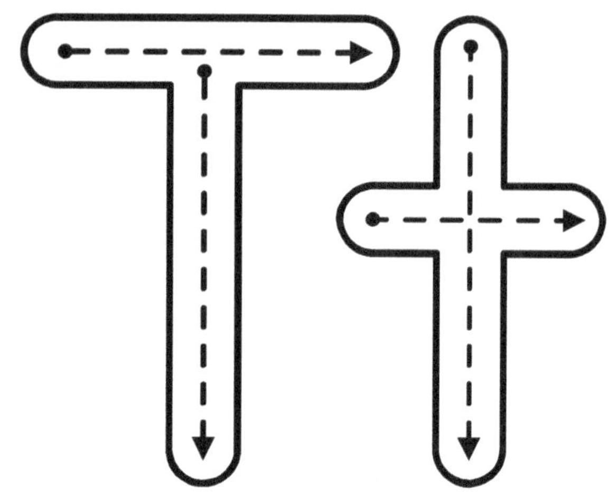

Trace The Letter - Tt

Circle The Letter - T

P D T O

R M I Q

V N S U

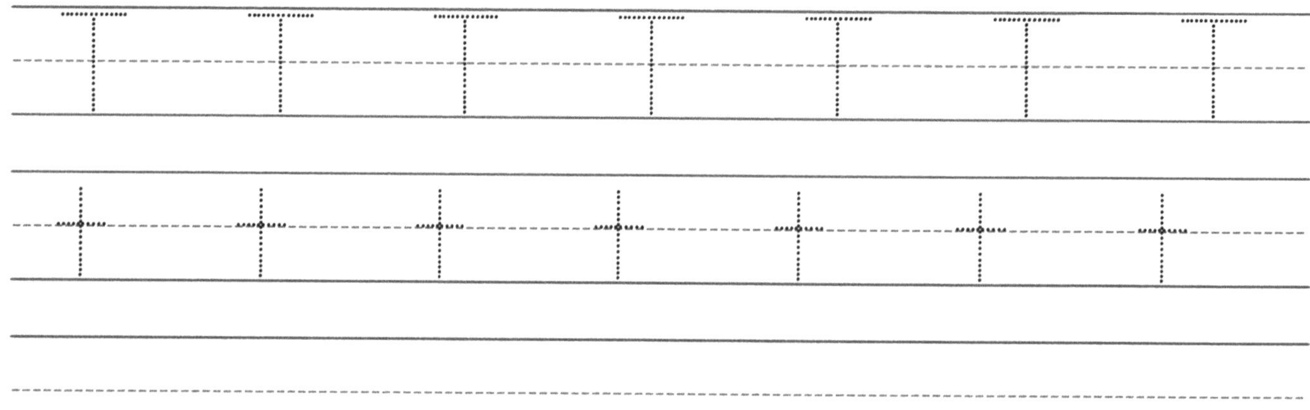

Write The Missing Letter

   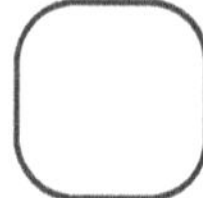

M N O P

Q R S

U V W X

Color And Trace

Train

<table><tr><td>A B C</td><td>PRACTICE TIME</td></tr></table>

<table>
<tr><td>

A B C

</td><td>

TRACING ALPHABETS

</td></tr>
</table>

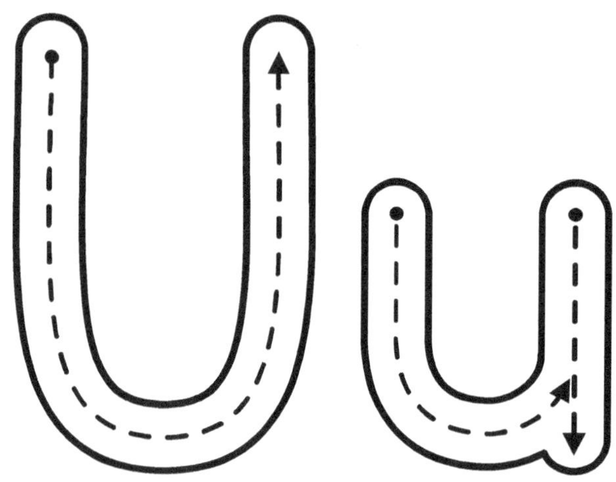

Trace The Letter - Uu

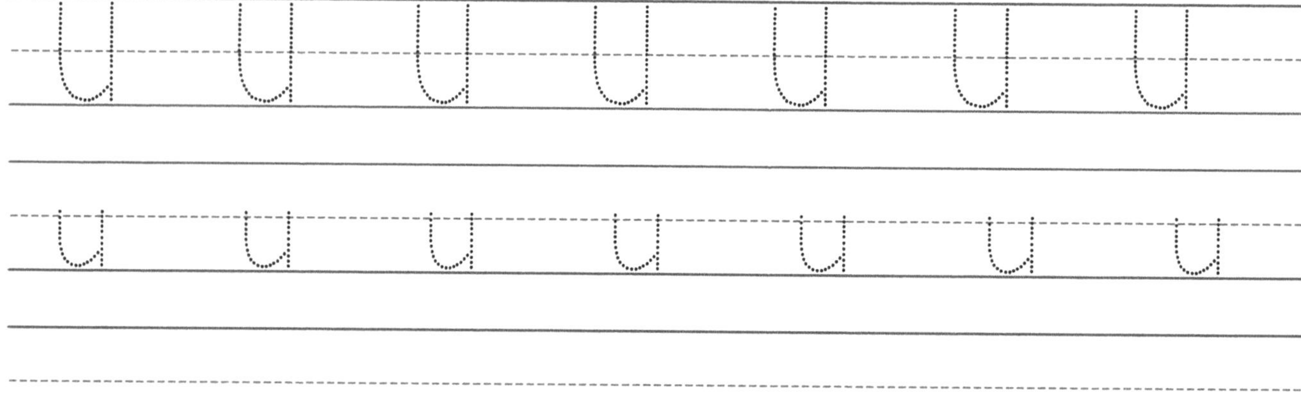

Circle The Letter - U

P	D	T	O
R	M	I	Q
V	N	S	U

Write The Missing Letter

M	N	O	P
Q	R	S	T
	V	W	X

Color And Trace

Umbrella

<table><tr><td>A B C</td><td>PRACTICE TIME</td></tr></table>

<table>
<tr><td>

A B C

</td><td>

TRACING ALPHABETS

</td></tr>
</table>

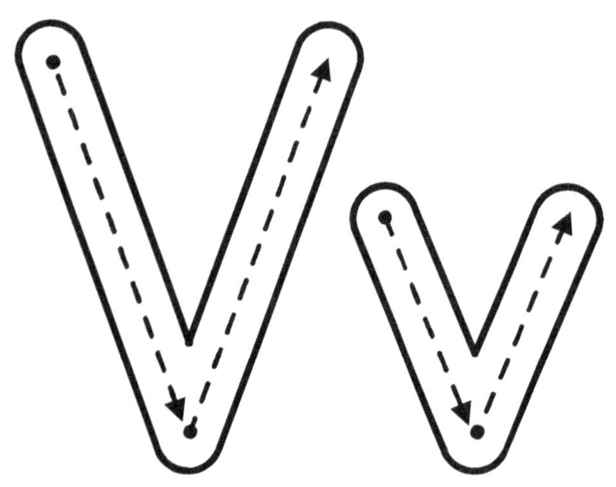

Trace The Letter - Vv

Write The Missing Letter

Color And Trace

Violin

Circle The Letter - W

P X T Z
R W I Q
Y N S U

Trace The Letter - Ww

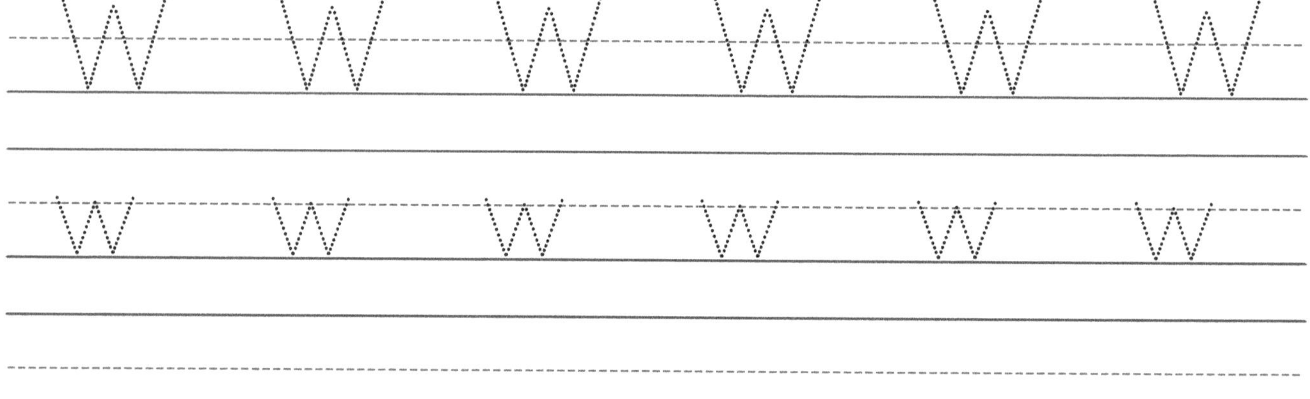

Write The Missing Letter

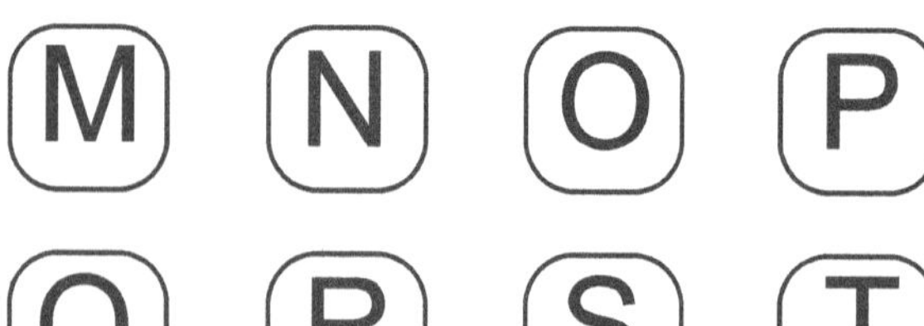

Color And Trace

Wolf

<table><tr><td>A B C</td><td>PRACTICE TIME</td></tr></table>

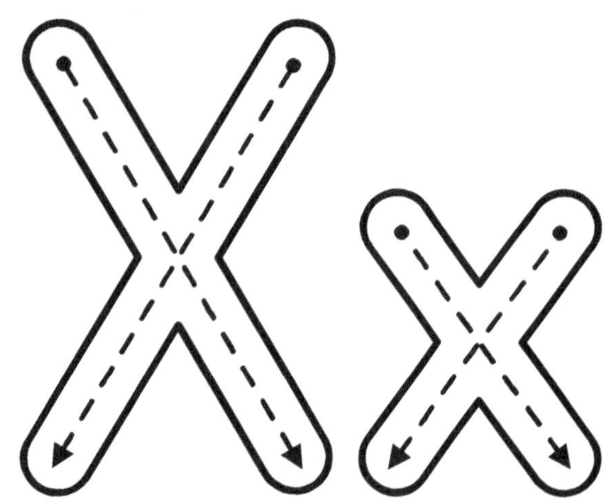

Trace The Letter - Xx

Circle The Letter - X

P X T Z
R W I Q
Y N S U

Write The Missing Letter

Color And Trace

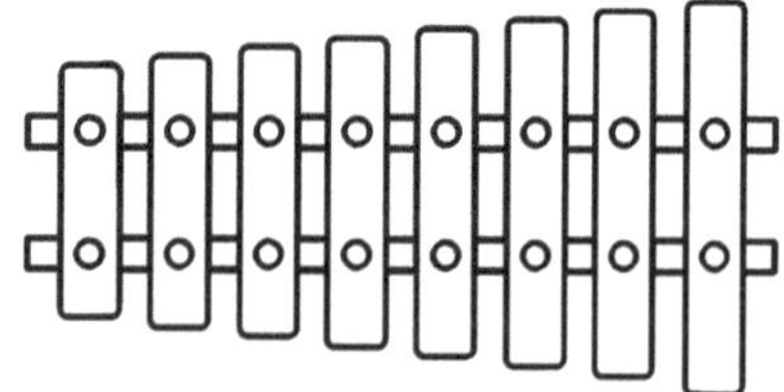
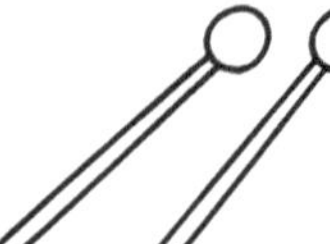

Xylophone

<table><tr><td>A B C</td><td># PRACTICE TIME</td></tr></table>

<table>
<tr><td>

A B C

</td><td>

TRACING ALPHABETS

</td></tr>
</table>

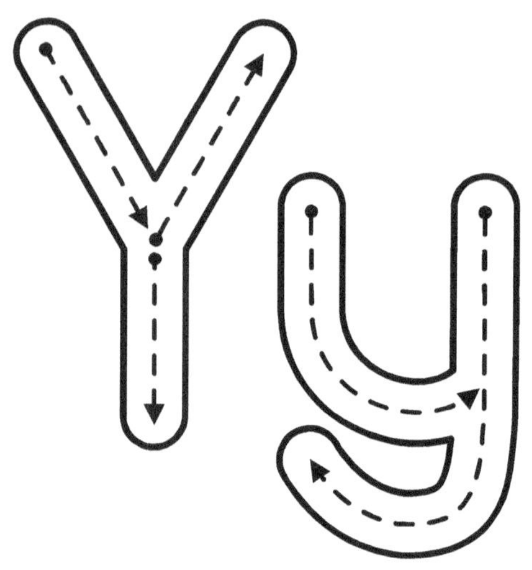

Trace The Letter - Yy

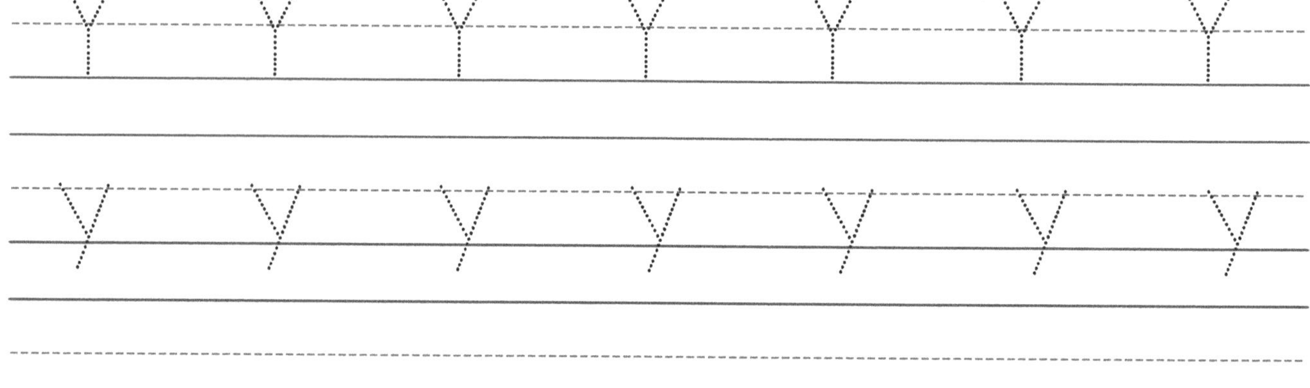

Circle The Letter - Y

E D T P
R Y I Q
X N S Z

Write The Missing Letter

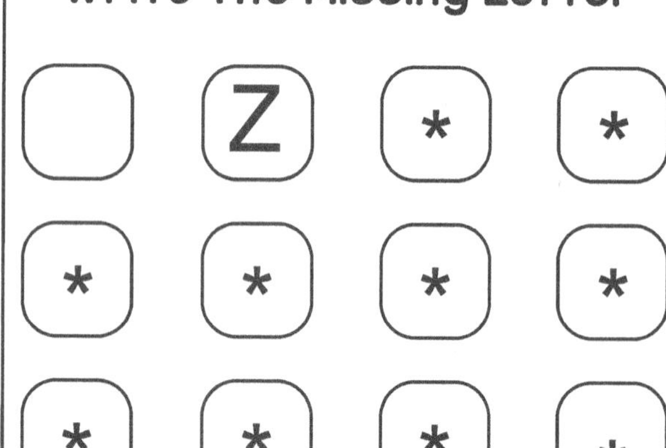

Color And Trace

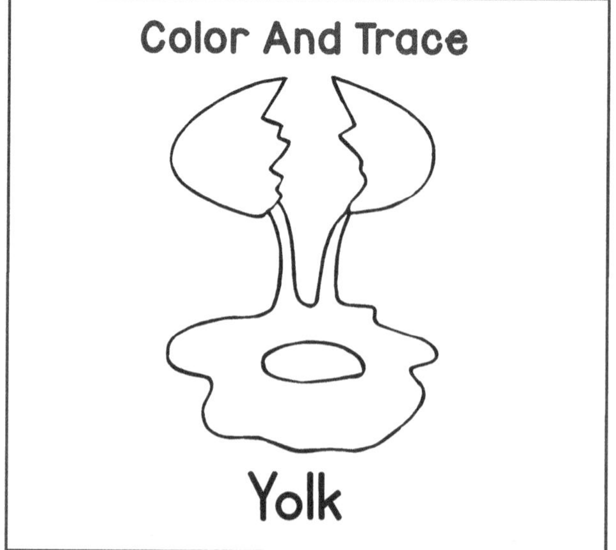

Yolk

<table><tr><td>A B C</td><td><h1>PRACTICE TIME</h1></td></tr></table>

TRACING ALPHABETS

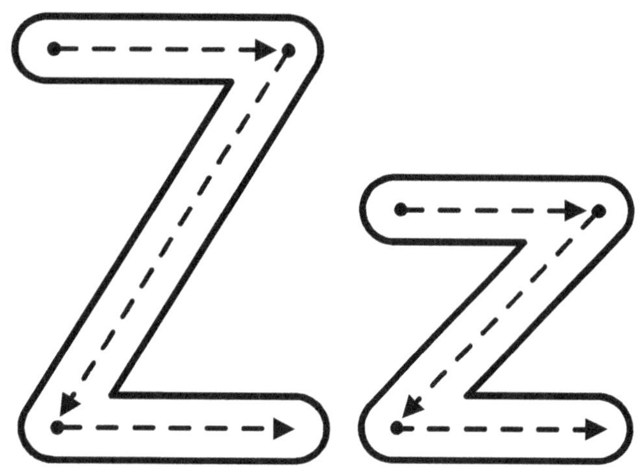

Trace The Letter - Zz

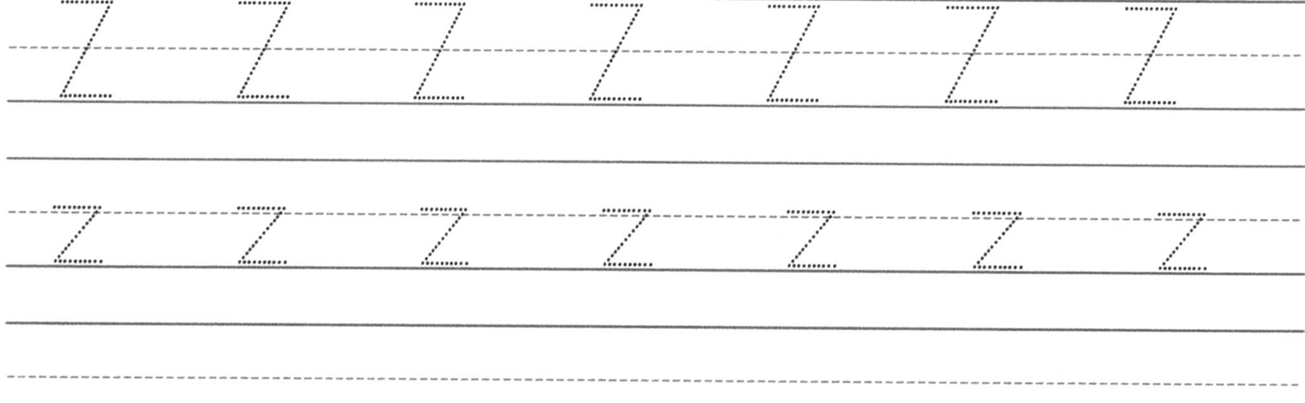

Write The Missing Letter

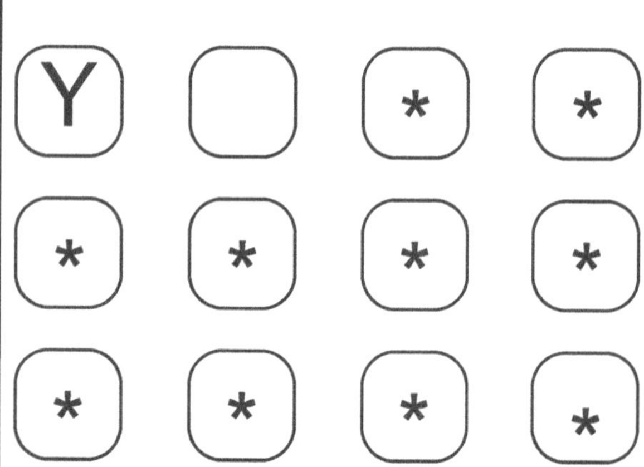

Color And Trace

Zebra

<table><tr><td>A B C</td><td>PRACTICE TIME</td></tr></table>

TRACING NUMBERS

TRACING NUMBERS

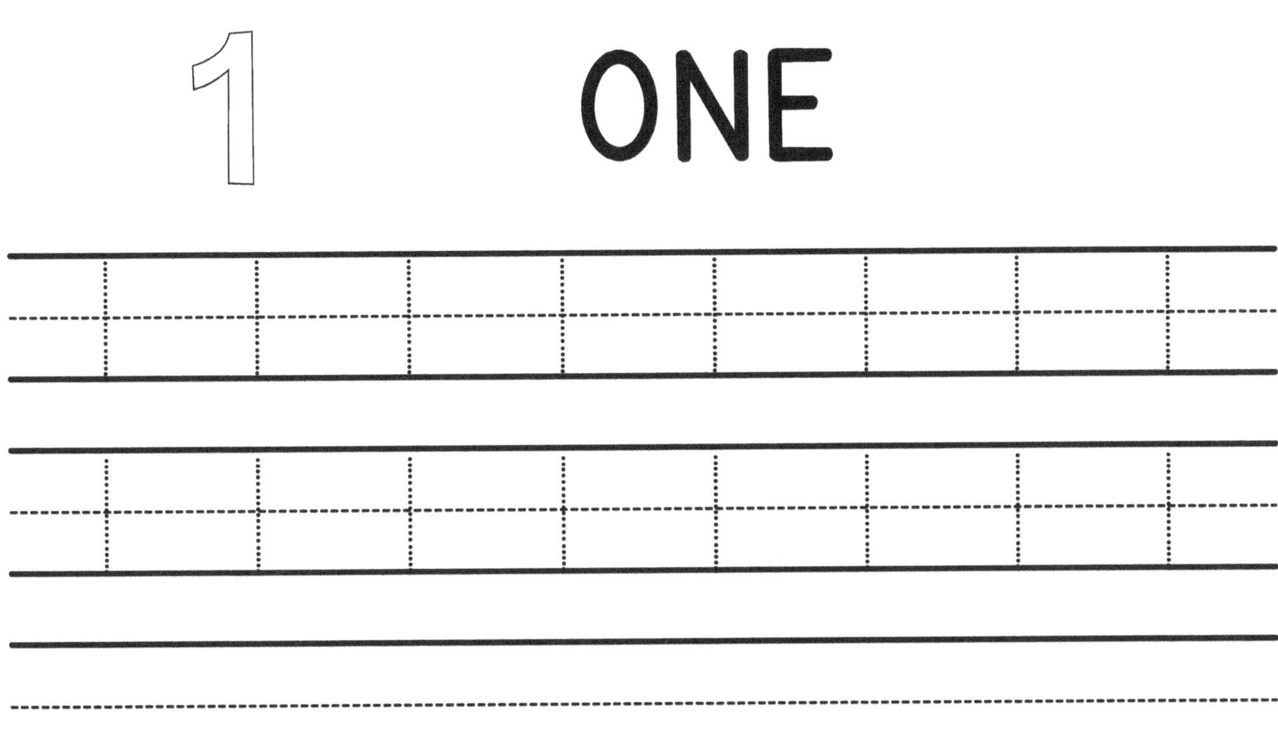

TRACING NUMBERS

THREE

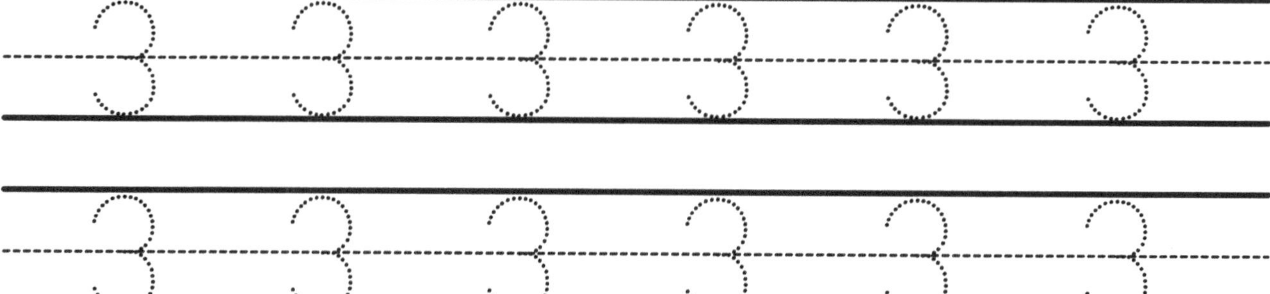

FOUR

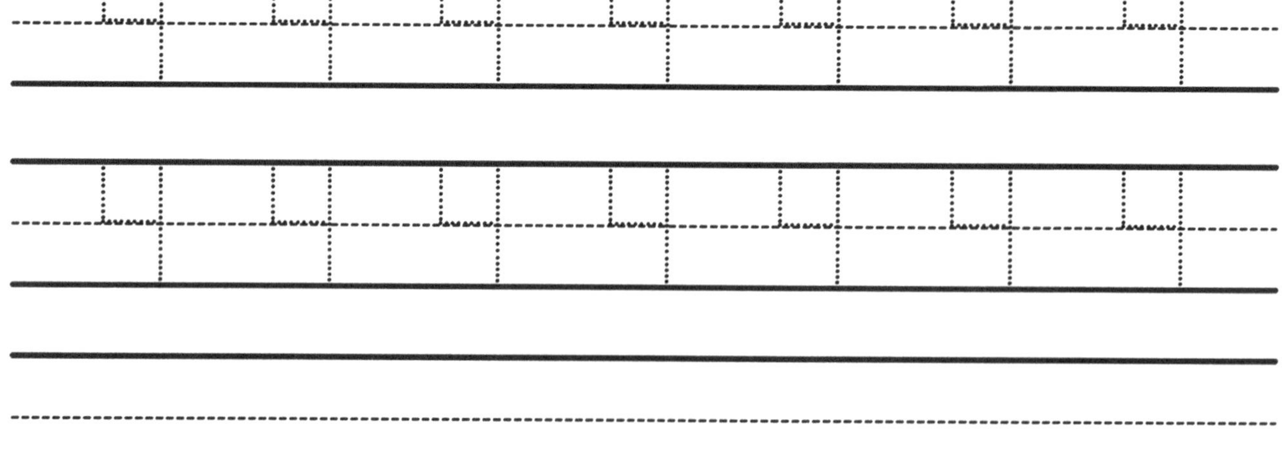

5 FIVE

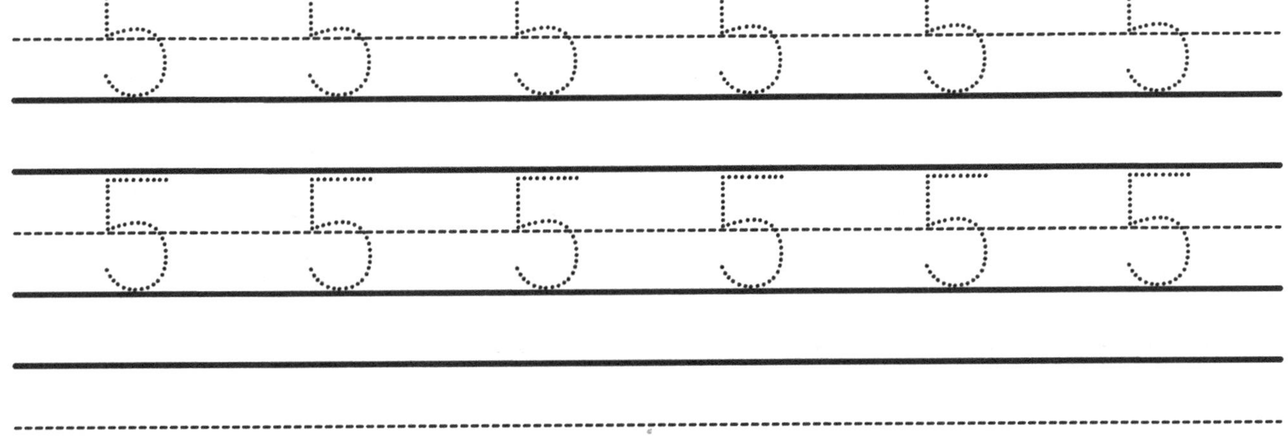

6 SIX

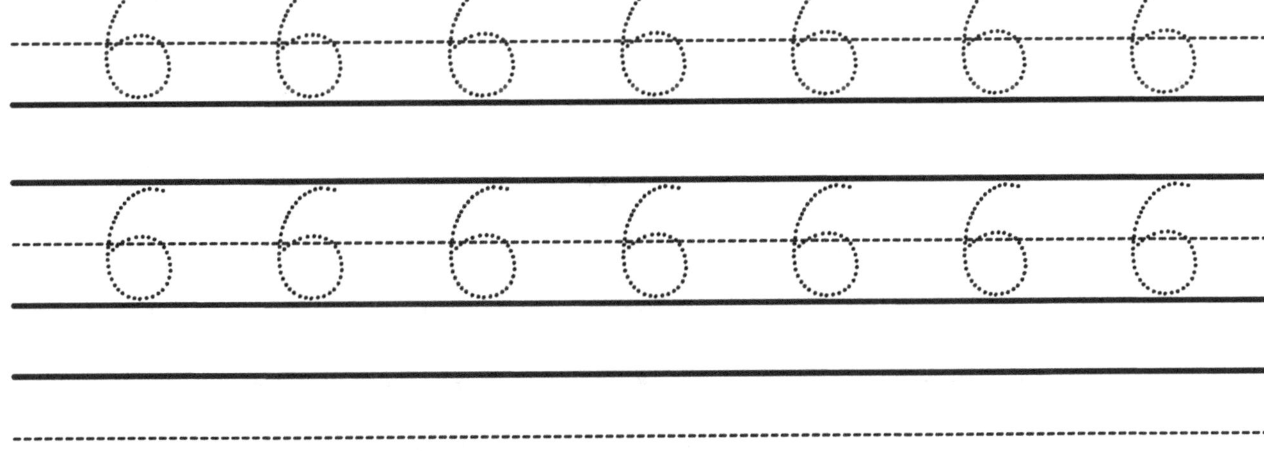

TRACING NUMBERS

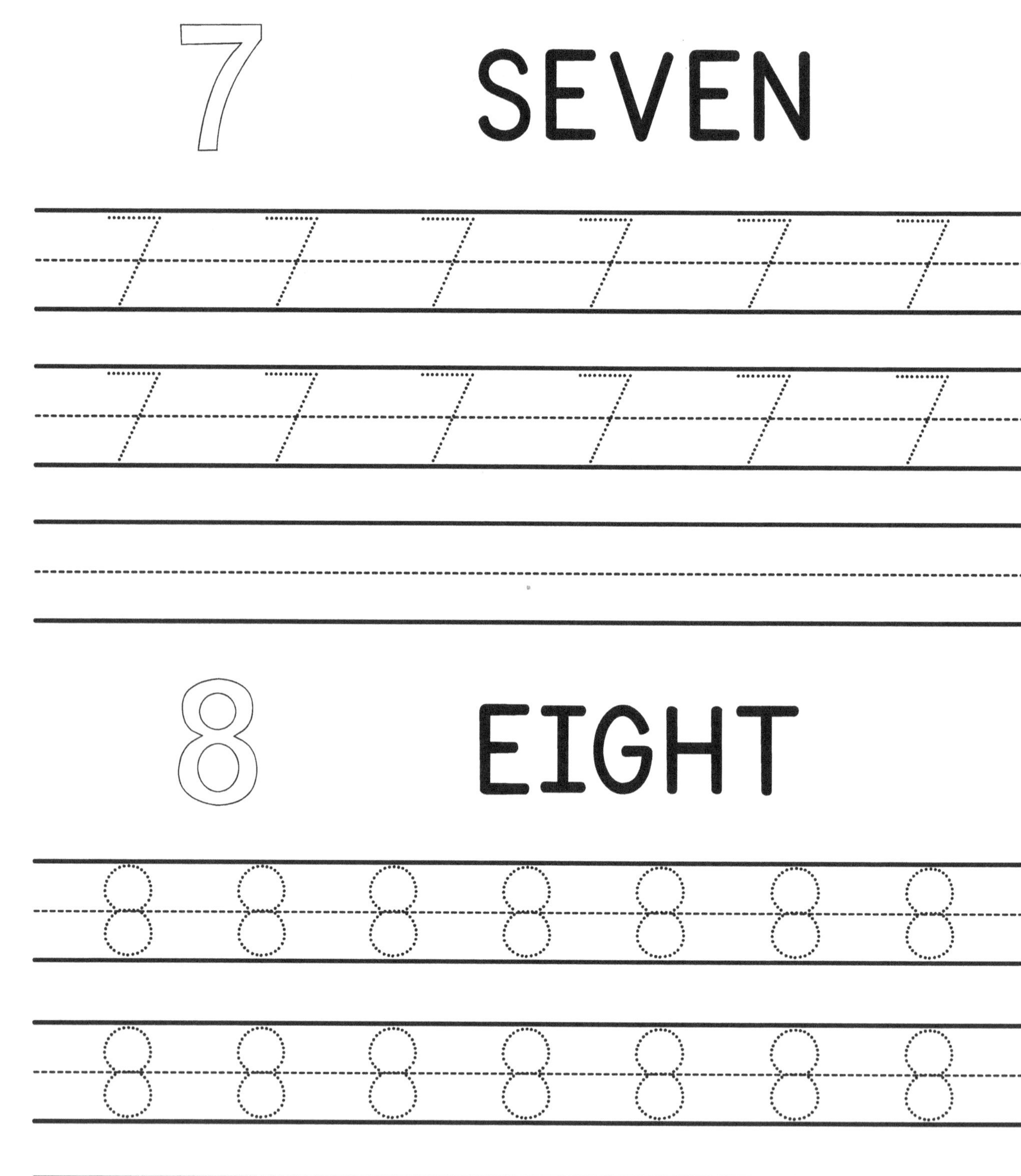

TRACING NUMBERS

NINE

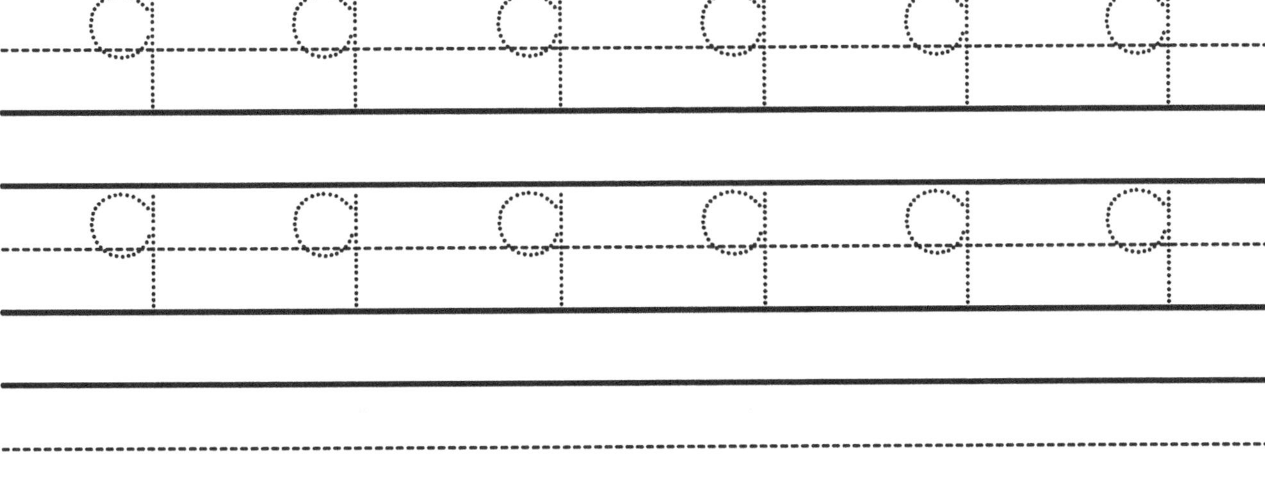

10   TEN

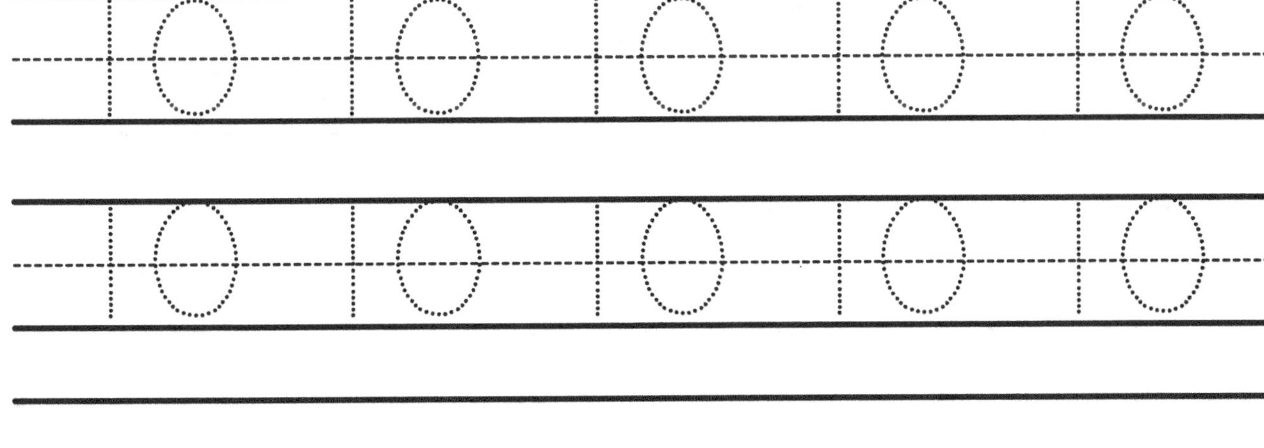

TRACING NUMBERS

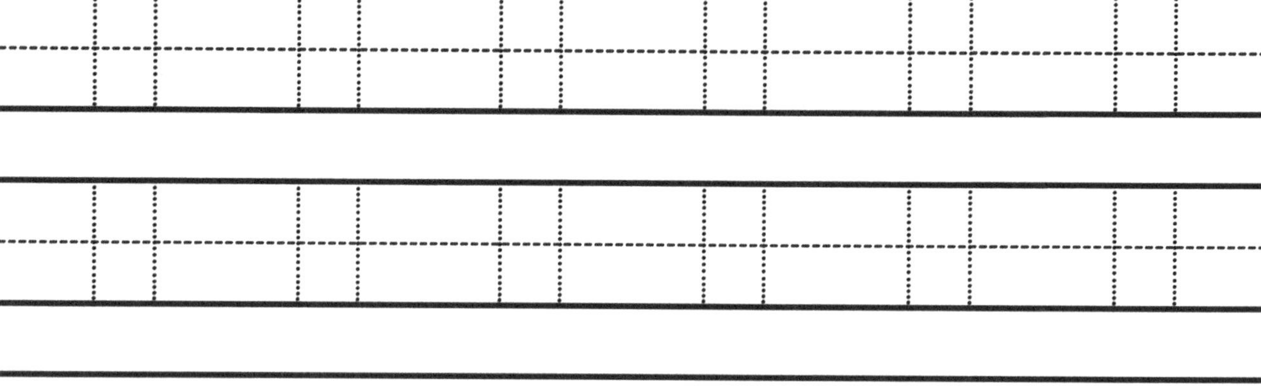

13 THIRTEEN

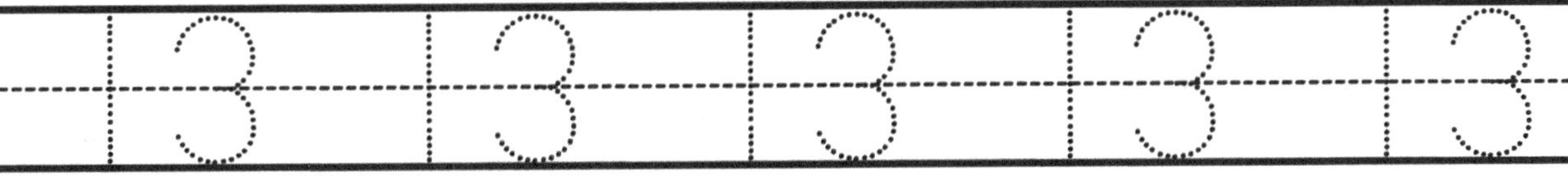

14 FOURTEEN

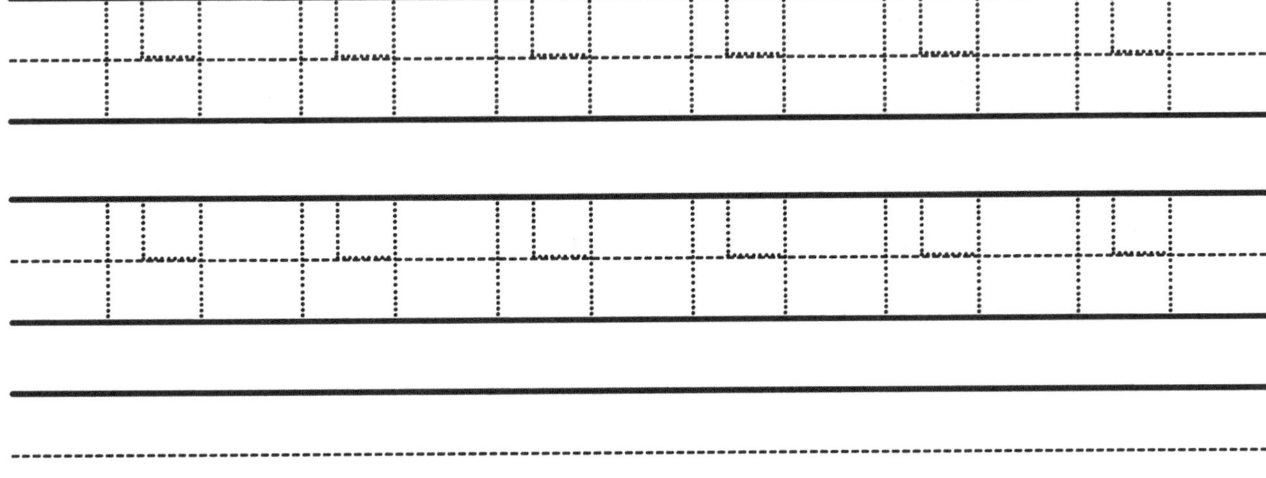

15 FIFTEEN

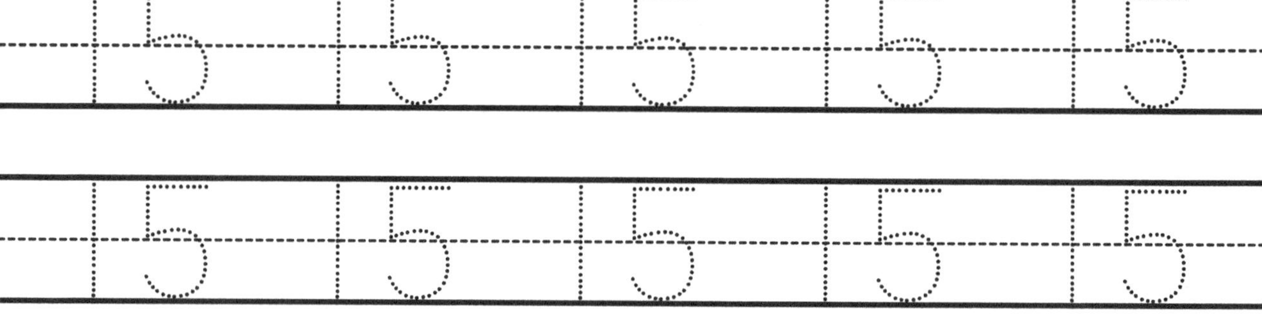

16 SIXTEEN

17 SEVENTEEN

18 EIGHTEEN

TRACING NUMBERS

NINETEEN

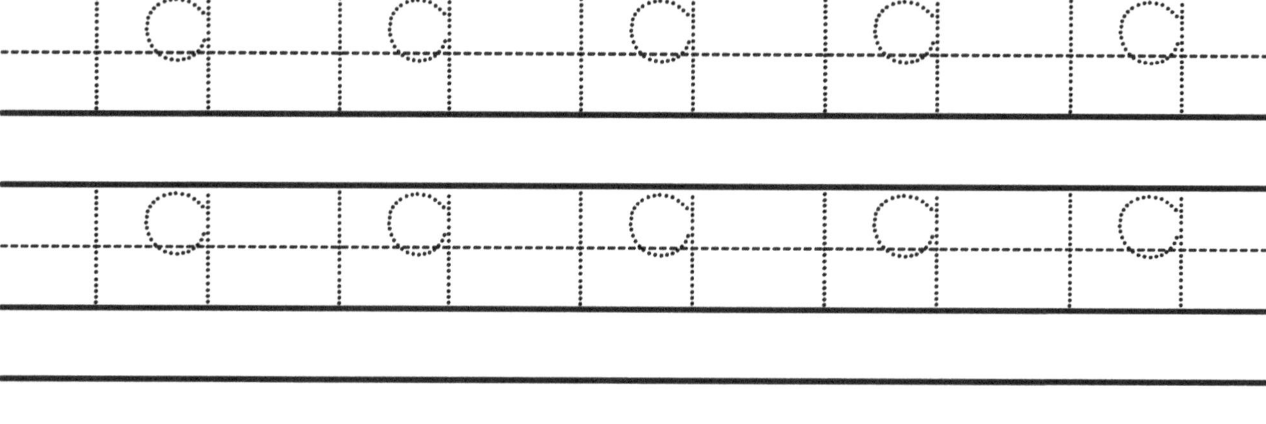

20 TWENTY

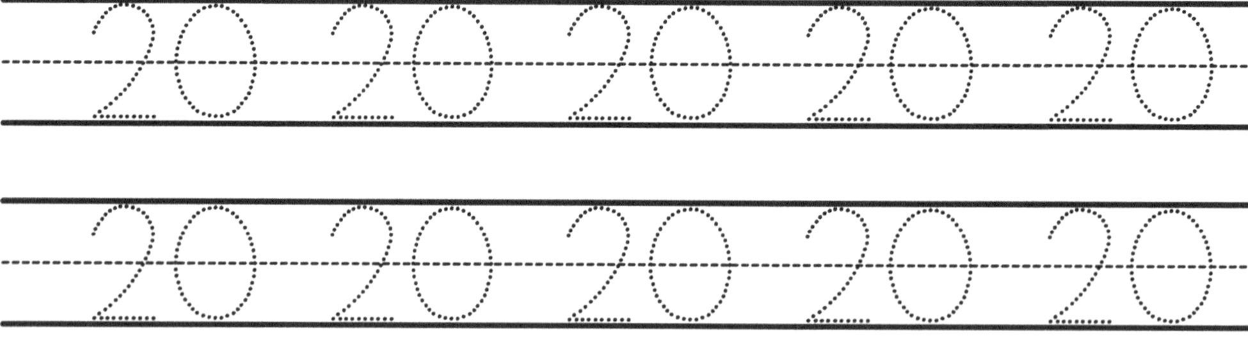

PRACTICE TIME

PRACTICE TIME

PRACTICE TIME

TRACING LINES

TRACING LINES

Trace the Line to Score a Goal

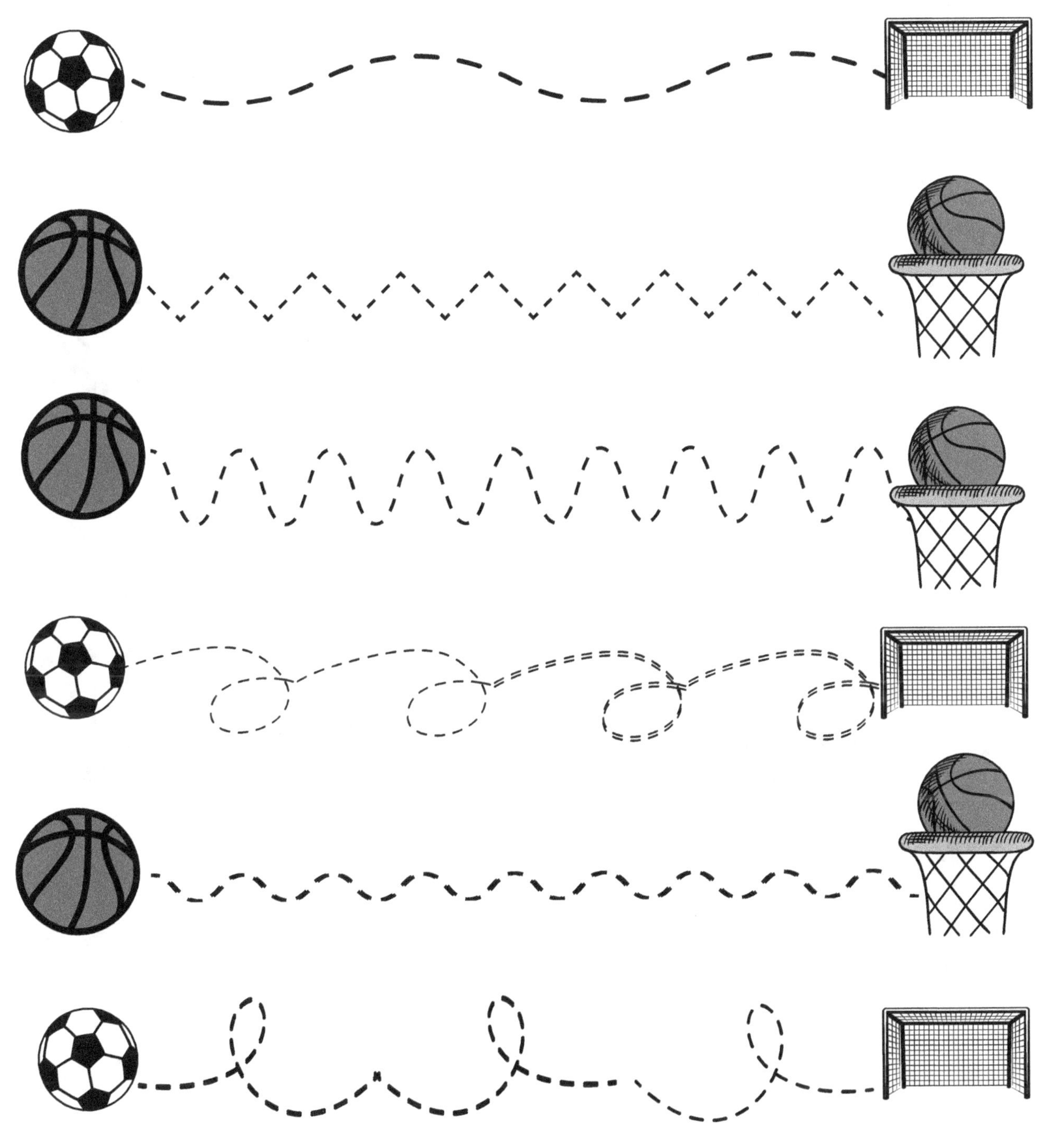

TRACING LINES

Save the little Cat

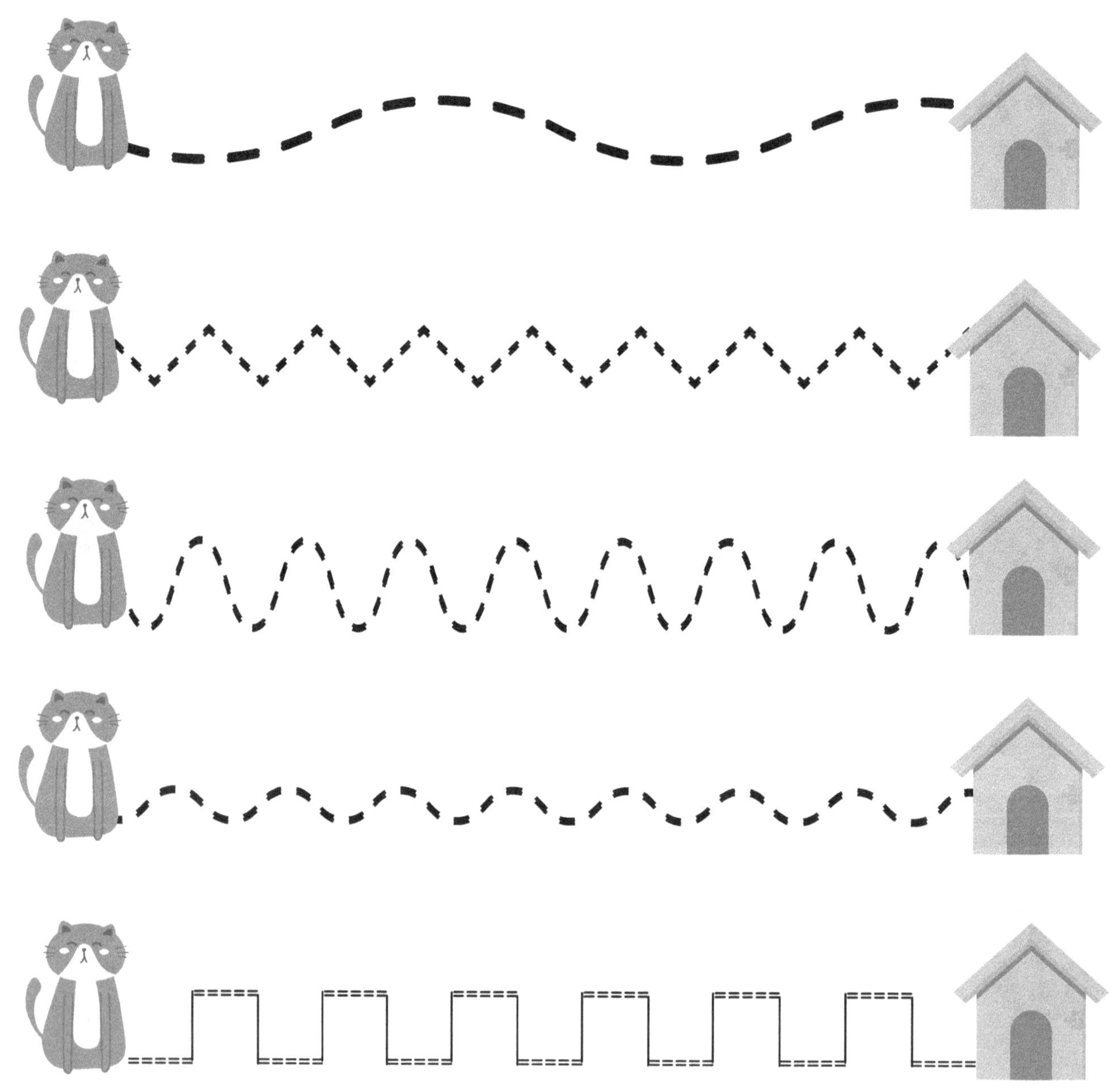

TRACING LINES

Win The Race

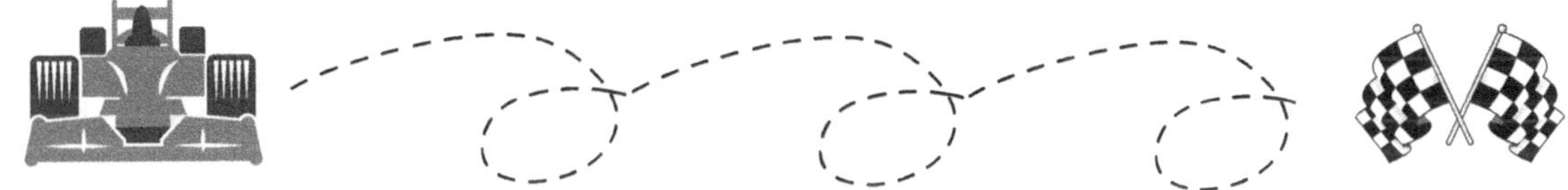

TRACING LINES

TRACING LINES

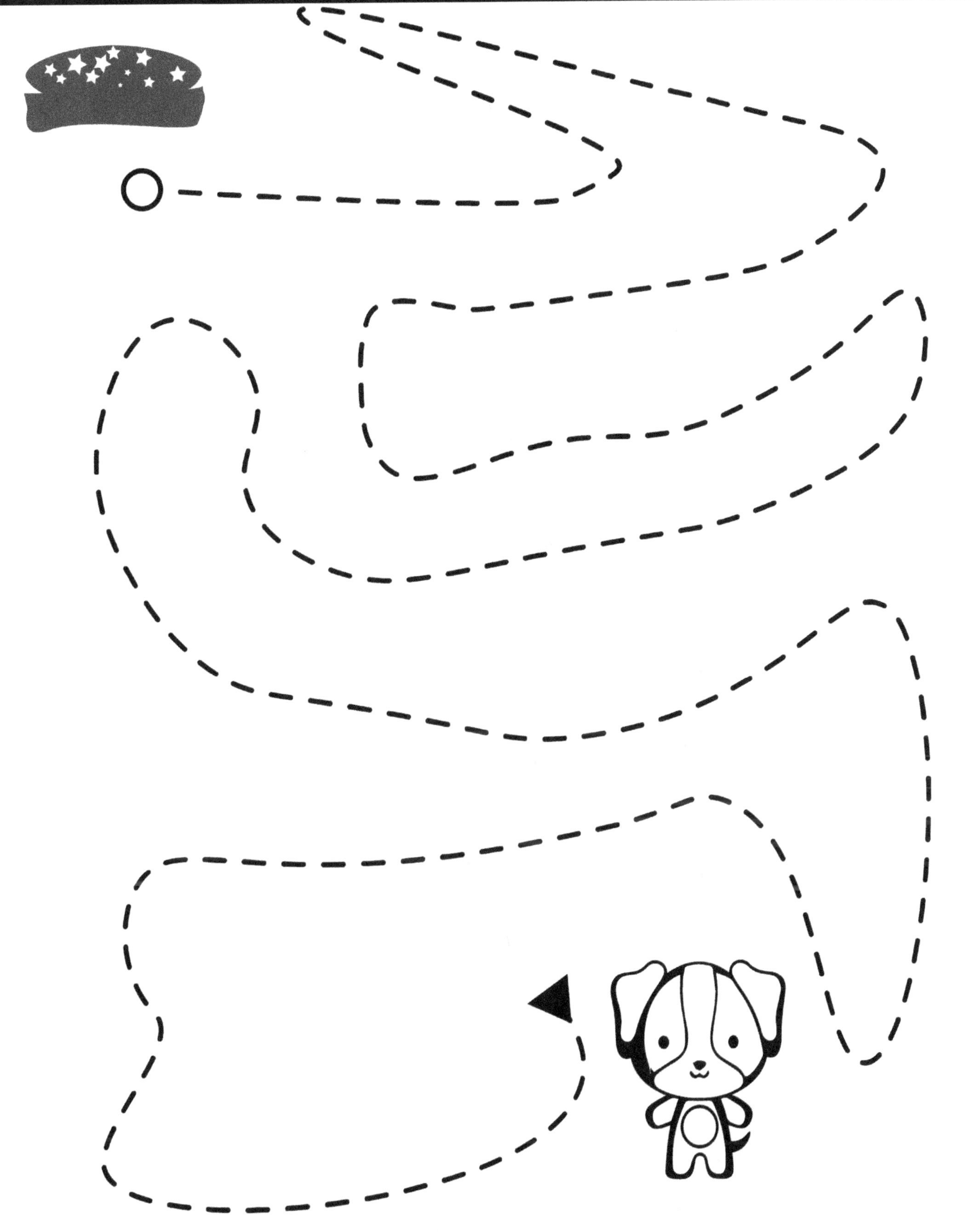

TRACING LINES

Circles

TRACING LINES

Triangle

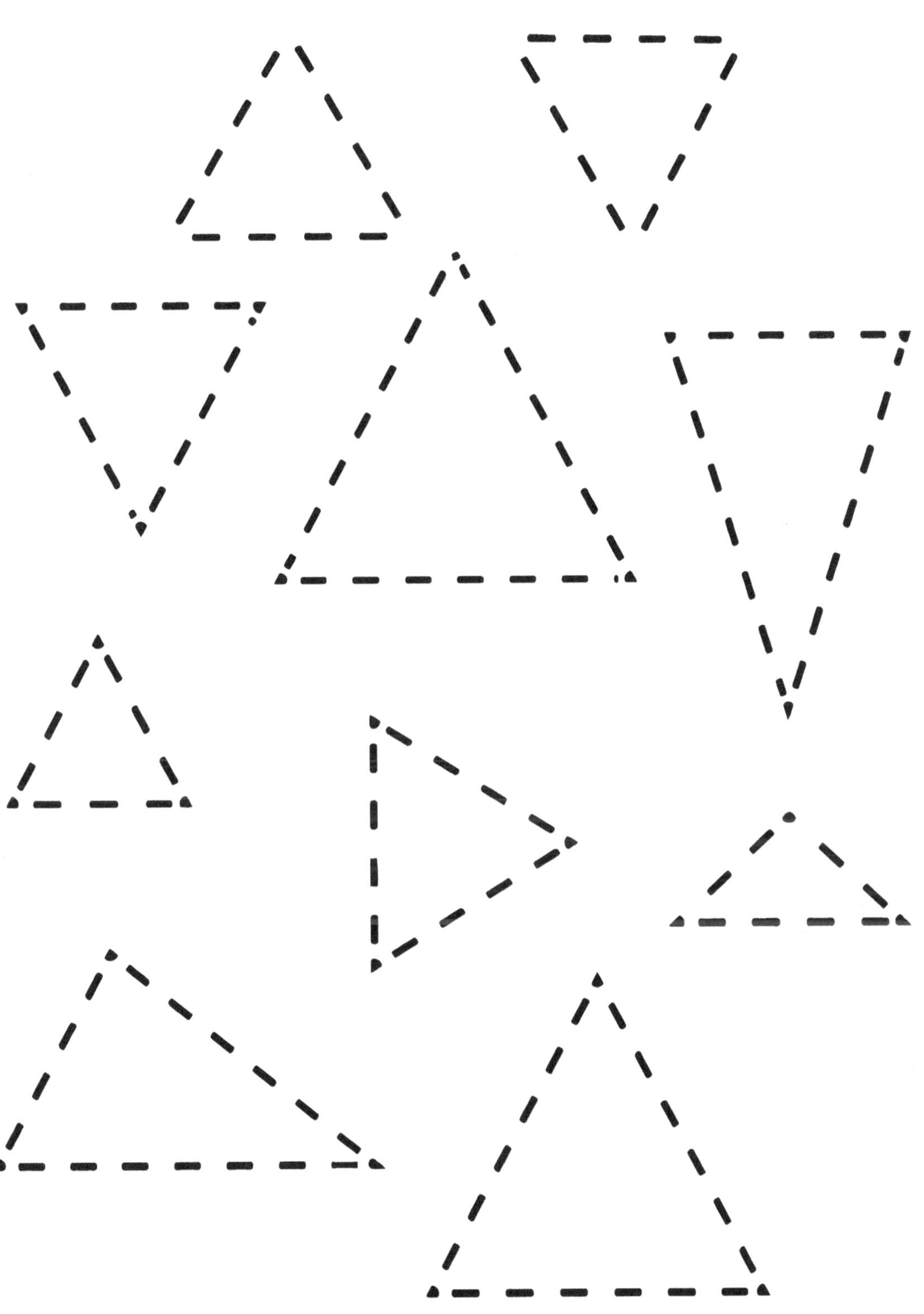

TRACING LINES

Square

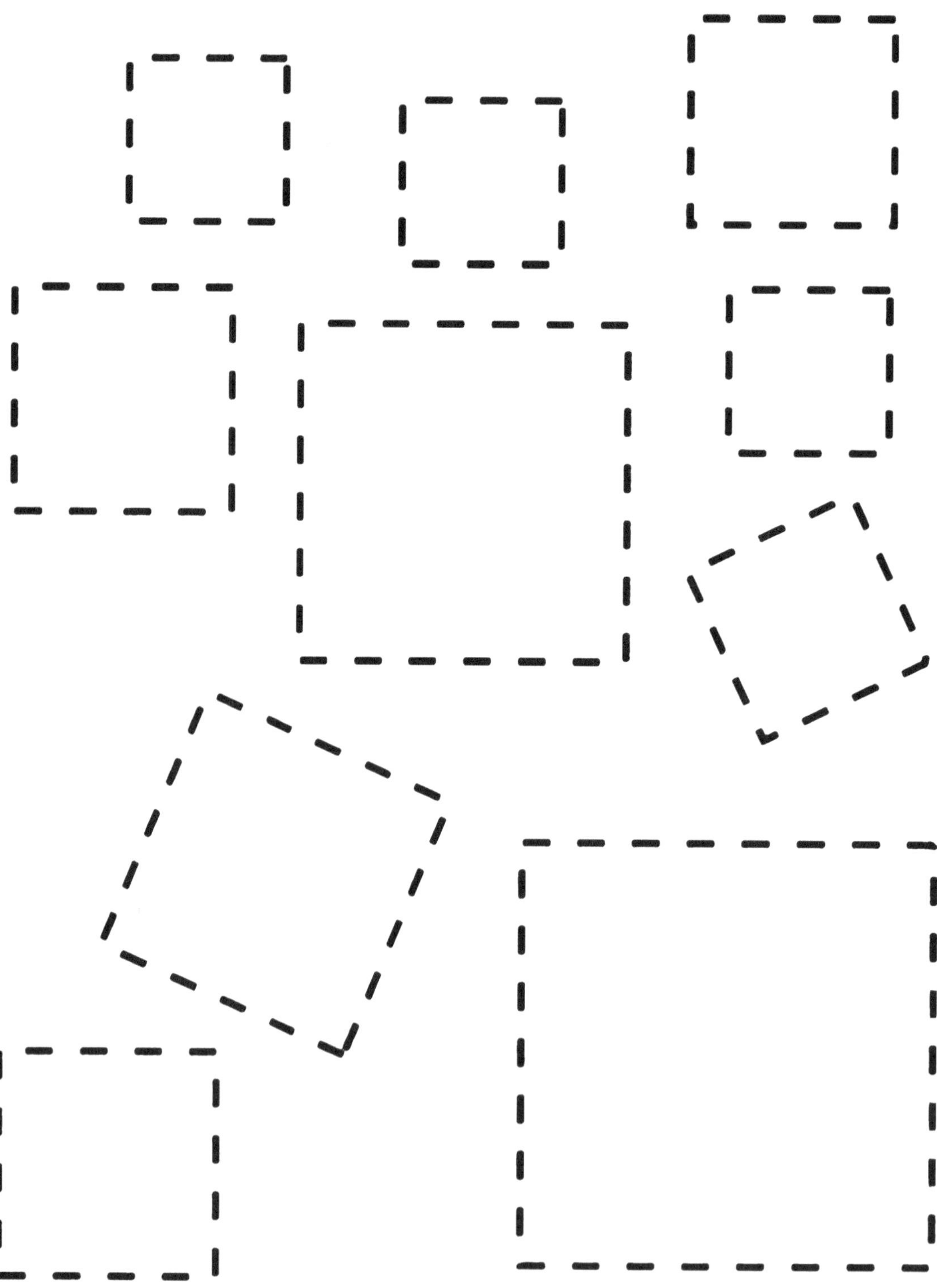

TRACING LINES

Rectangle

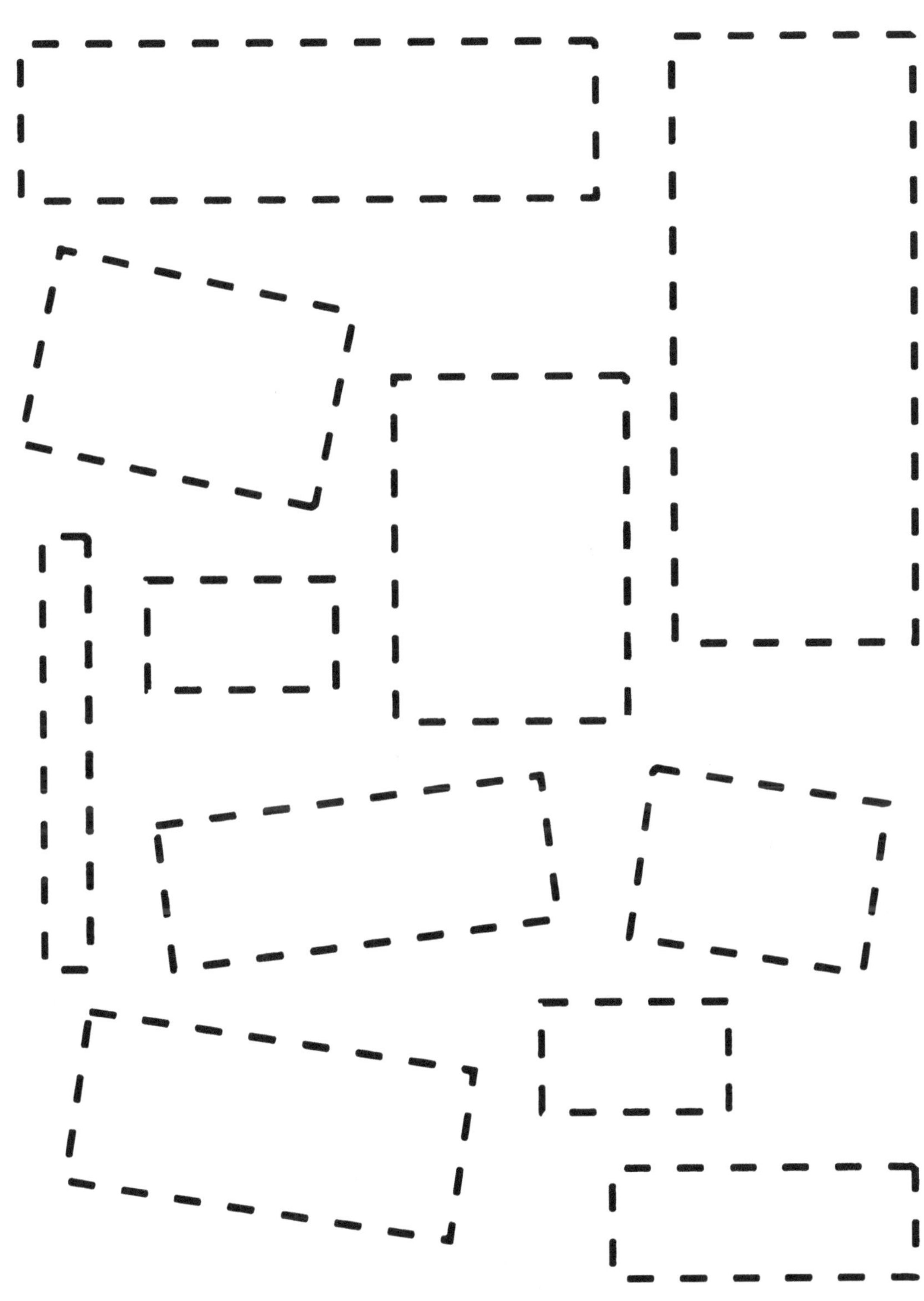

TRACING LINES

Diamond

CONNECT DOTS

TIGER

LION

MONKEY

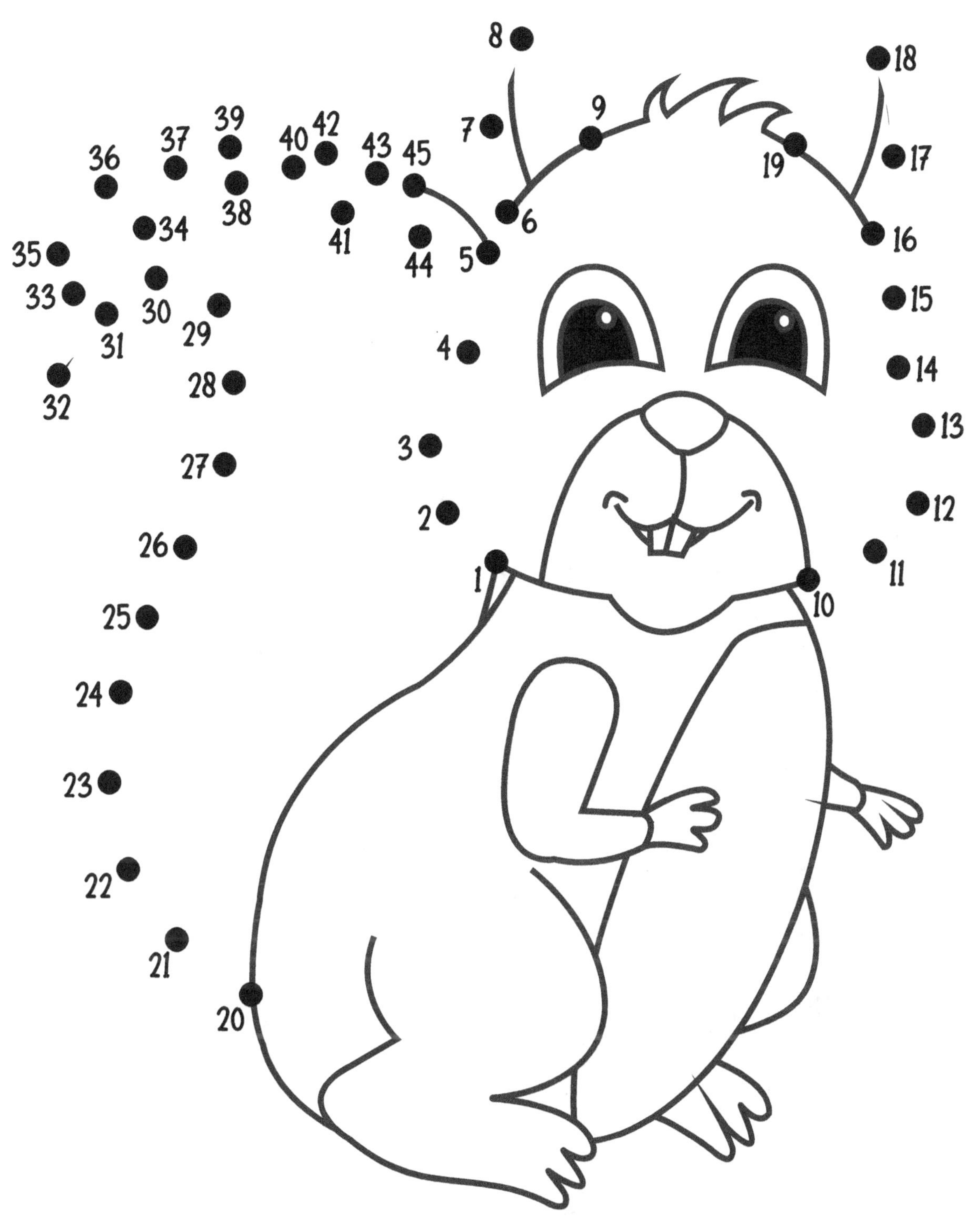

RABBIT

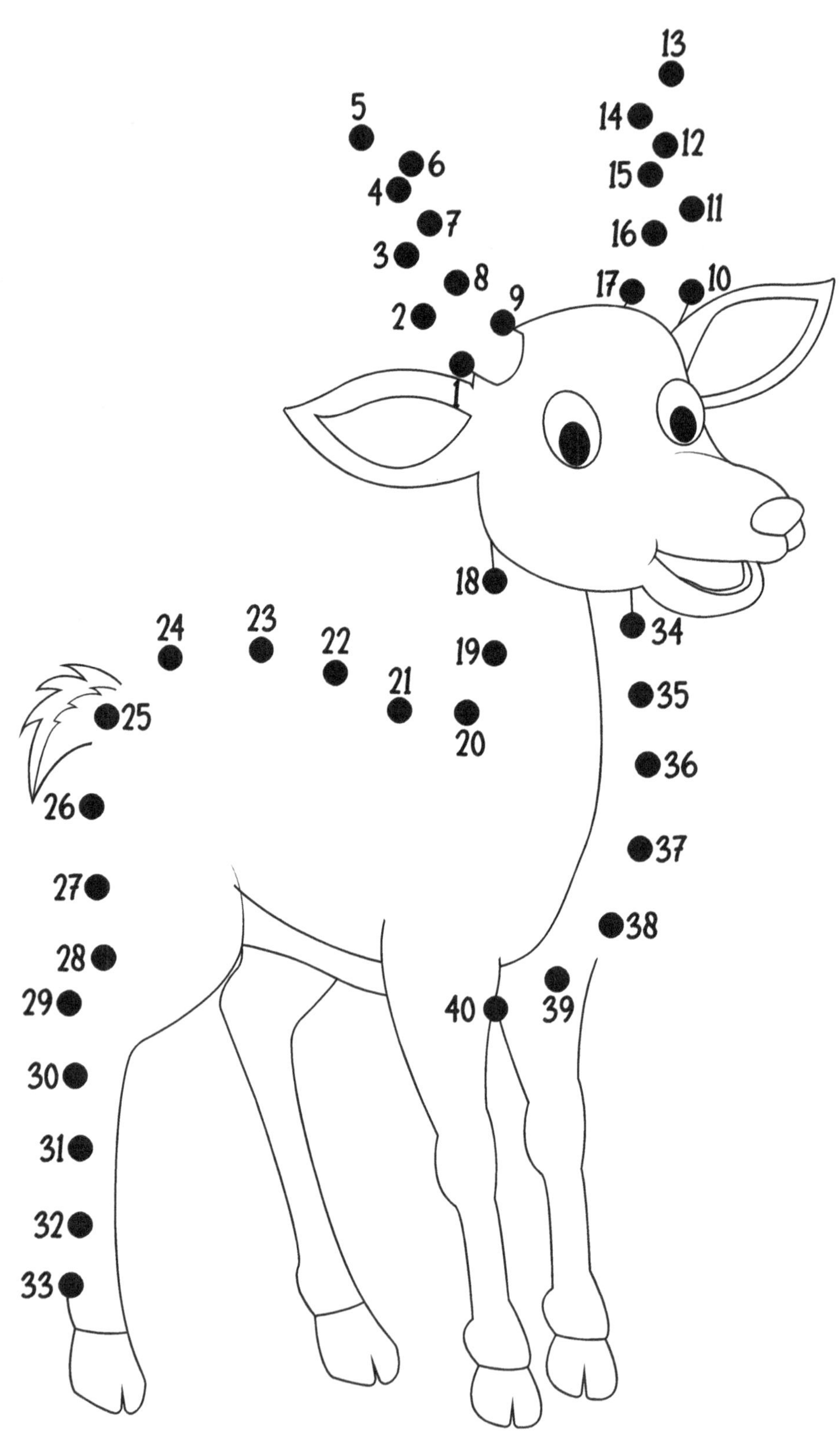

DEAR

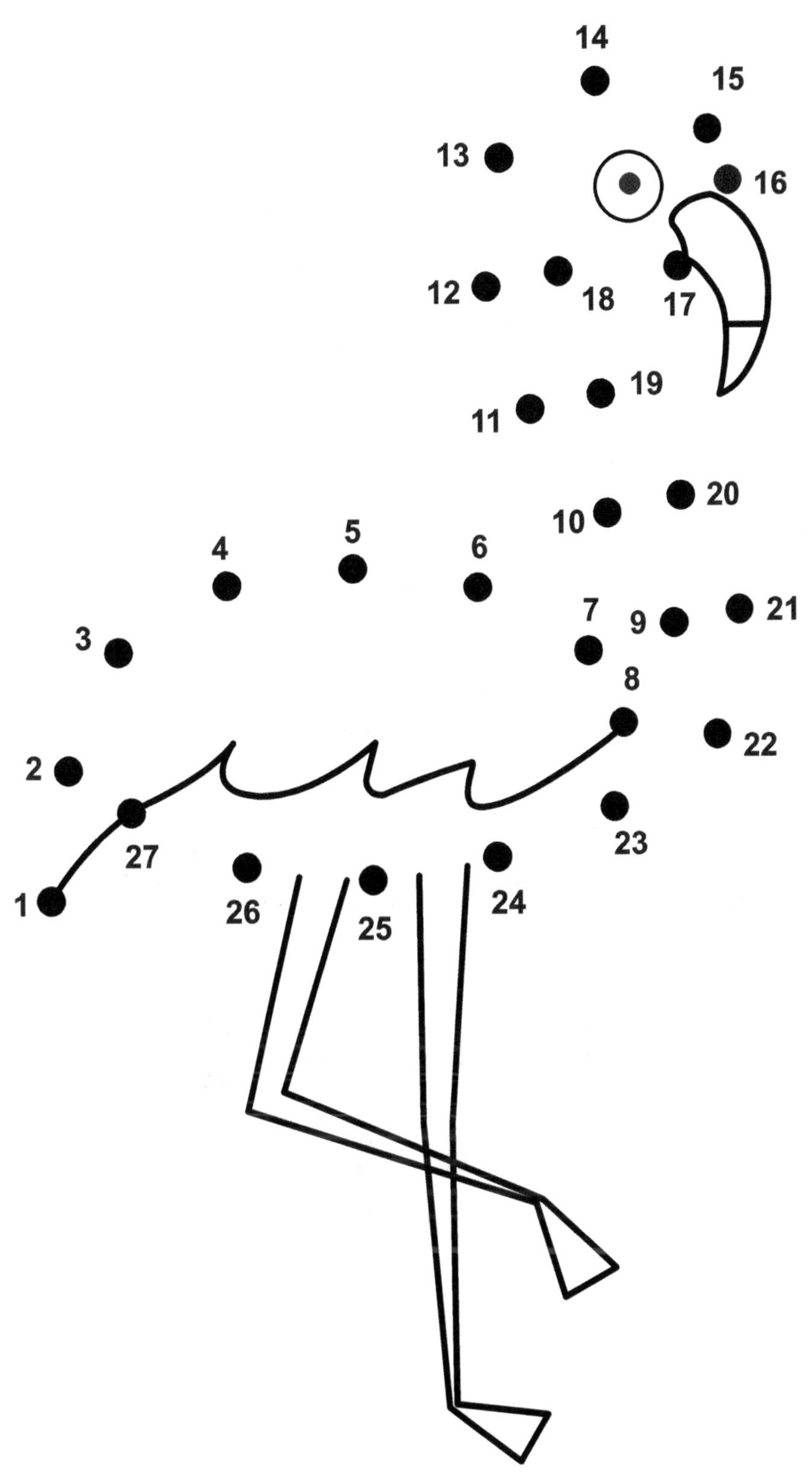

FLAMINGO

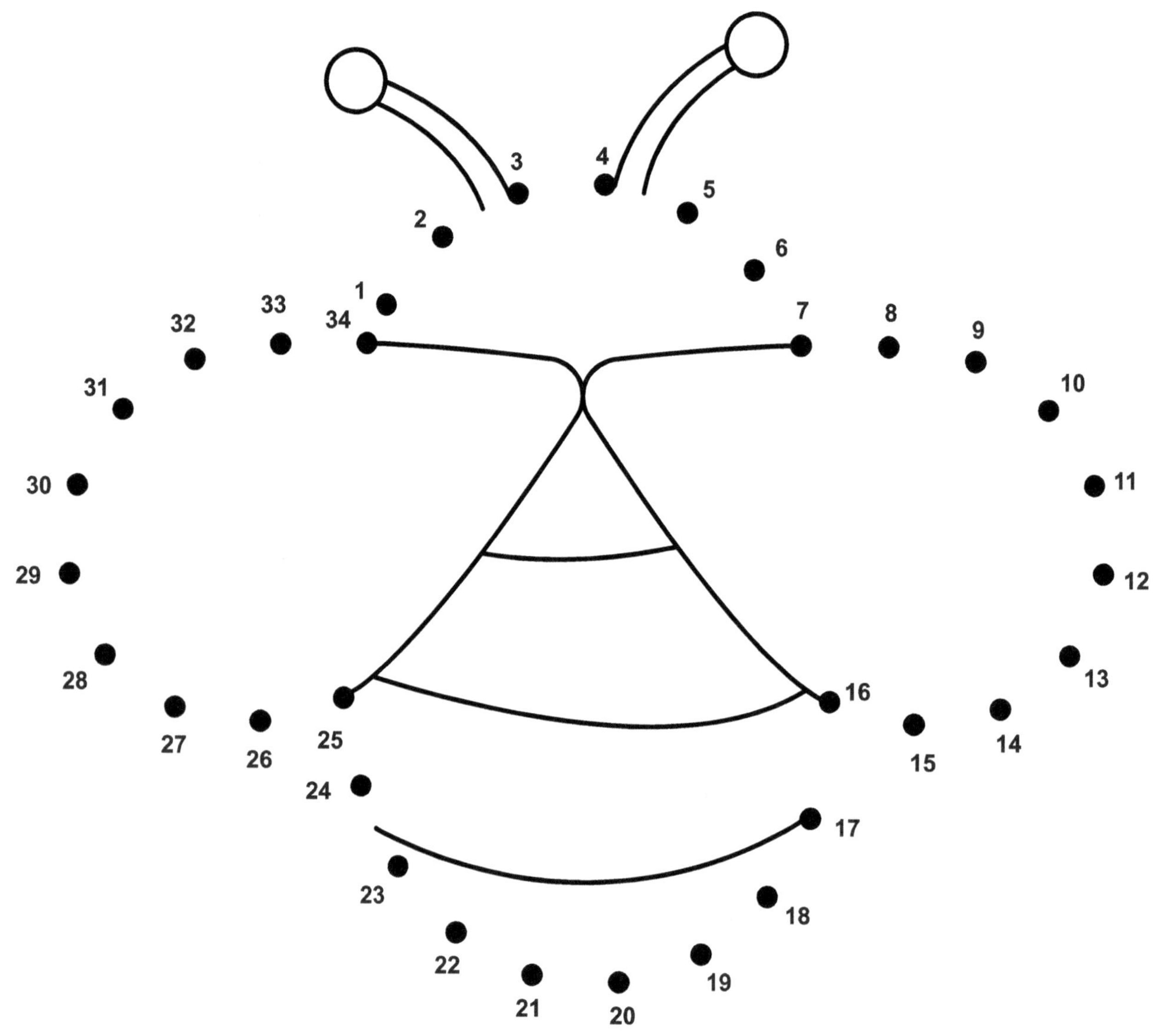

BEE

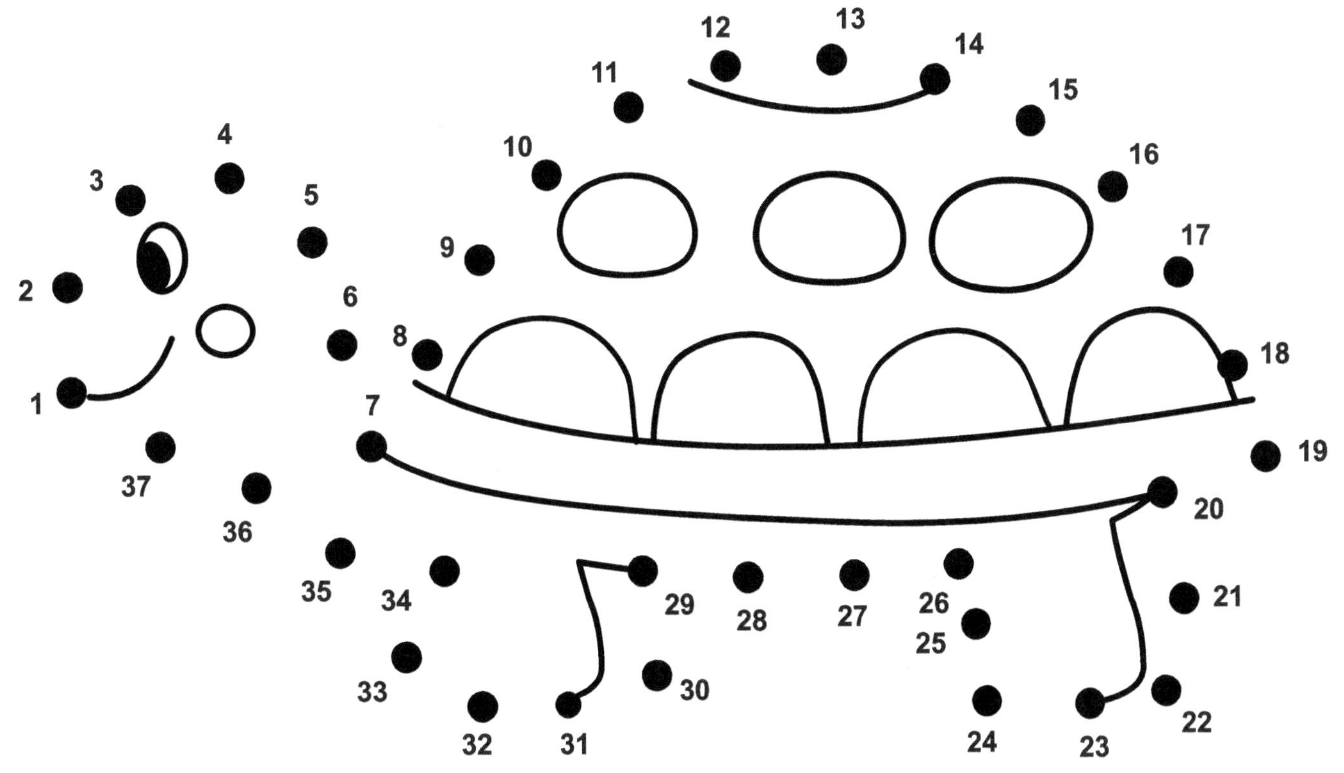

TURTLE

COLORING PAGE

APPLE

SHARK

PICKUP

CAT

ROCKET

CRAB

LION

APPLE

DRAGON

ELEPHANT

DOG

UNICORN

SHEEP

CANDY

TURTLE

This Certificate Is Presented To:

Date

Signature